Praise for *Tributaries*

"Ryan Brod has performed a magic trick with this excellent collection, combining an old-school heart with a contemporary head. The stories in *Tributaries* beautifully capture the thrill, the poignancy and the magic of a life centered on the woods and water."
—Monte Burke, author of *Lords of the Fly* and *Saban*

"Hunting and fishing exude a power source ultimately challenging you beyond measure, ensuring you'll remain resilient and forever young. In *Tributaries,* Ryan Brod shares his vast spectrum of a wonderful life well-lived."
—Andy Mill, Olympian, champion fly fisherman, author of *A Passion for Tarpon*

"Brod's passion and respect for the creatures, their habitat and dignity, infuse each page with his lyrical prose. Luxuriant with detail, these essays usher the reader toward the intersection of flora, fauna, family, and friendship. Ultimately, *Tributaries* leaves us with a deeper awareness of our own personal ecosystems."
—Catharine Murray, author of *Now You See the Sky*

TRIBUTARIES

Also from Islandport Press

Suddenly, the Cider Didn't Taste So Good
John Ford

Backtrack
V. Paul Reynolds

Bald Eagles, Bear Cubs, and Hermit Bill
Ron Joseph

A Full Net
Susan Daignault

Whatever It Takes
May Davidson

Tales From Misery Ridge
Paul J. Fournier

Maine Trivia
Dean Lunt and John McDonald

Nine Mile Bridge
Helen Hamlin

In Maine
John N. Cole

Ghost Buck
Dean Bennett

TRIBUTARIES

Essays from Woods and Waters

Ryan Brod

ISLANDPORT PRESS

ISLANDPORT PRESS

Islandport Press
P.O. Box 10
Yarmouth, Maine 04096
www.islandportpress.com
info@islandportpress.com

First Edition: October 2023
Printed in the United States of America.
All photographs, unless otherwise noted, courtesy of Ryan Brod.

ISBN: 978-1-952143-76-2
Library of Congress Control Number: 2023946755

Dean L. Lunt | Editor-in-Chief, Publisher
Shannon M. Butler | Vice President
Emily A. Lunt | Book Designer
Cover Designer | Lucian Burg/LUDesign Studios
Cover Artist | Frederick Stivers
Author Photo by Nora Saks

For my family.

"When it is time to leave this place of return, what will I say that I found here?"

—Joy Harjo

TABLE OF CONTENTS

PROLOGUE

It started with a red and white bobber. I loved the way, just after a take, the bobber twitched, white side skyward like an eyeball, then vanished beneath the surface. This was how I spent boyhood summers—fishing nightcrawlers or golden shiners beneath a bobber on the Serpentine River, in Smithfield, Maine. My grandparents, Anne and Al, owned a small red cabin there with a screened-in porch and a bell my grandmother used to call me in for dinner. The river was really a bog: milfoil choking the waterway by early summer, no current to speak of. I didn't consider the water quality until my sister, Emily, and I jumped in one hot summer's afternoon and emerged covered in slime and duck weed. Grandpa Al, who had once worked on submarines in a Great Lakes' shipyard, kept a leaky rowboat at the dock. He fished occasionally but preferred to tinker on land. Every now and then he'd take me out for a row. I remember the squeak of the oar locks as he paddled. Once, rowing us back to the dock after a brief and unsuccessful afternoon of fishing, he stopped to whack an overgrown snapping turtle with the blunt end of his oar.

The Serpentine held impressive largemouth bass, living amongst fallen timber, around lily pads, beneath abandoned, crumbling docks like the one I used to fish from.

I loved baseball, too. I stole rocks from my grandparents' short driveway to hit them into or, occasionally, over the Serpentine. As a bat, I used discarded table legs Grandpa Al—an avid woodworker—had salvaged. I got good at stealing a few rocks at a time, so he wouldn't notice bald spots in the driveway, though he must have known, must have heard wood striking rock, the mechanical *whuuurrrr*-ing noise when I fouled one off, or my hollers when I finally connected, launching a moon shot over resident bass and into the woods across the river.

I was good at baseball, at first. I made the All-Star teams, hit home runs, threw a twelve-to-six curveball that made batters flinch. Later, in high school, I changed my windup, then hurt my pitching arm. I lost control of the strike zone, got the yips, couldn't, as they say, hit the broad side of a barn. My high leg kick at the plate made me late on fastballs, so I couldn't make up for it at the plate. I lost confidence and spent time on the bench.

It was this event—my ugly break-up with baseball—that activated my dive into fishing, or, at least, that's the story I tell myself, the one that makes the most sense, in retrospect.

I fished alone a lot. This is not to say I was a loner; I fished frequently with my father, and with my good friend, Evan, and some of my best childhood memories involved big bass in a shared canoe just before or after summer sunsets. Mosquitoes stole blood and I didn't care. I was so attuned to my surroundings, so happy to be there that I could have lost a pint of blood without noticing.

But fishing alone allowed me time to think, and fishing offered a new and challenging arena in which I could become as proficient as I wanted. I cast my blaze orange floating Rapala beside a stump, twitched it, then waited. There was a lot of waiting. A lot of nothing happening. My moods spiked and dipped according to my success (or lack thereof) on the water.

I tied knots that failed, caught more trees than I could count, missed hook sets, hooked myself, buried a treble into my sister's thigh that needed surgical extraction (sorry, Em).

I was told by those around me—my mother in particular—that I felt things more than other people did. I remember my father saying, not infrequently, "You're so *sensitive*" in moments of frustration, his emphasis on the word undermining my feeling that something about me, something I didn't choose, was quite wrong, maybe uncorrectable. My mother sometimes countered by reminding me I just felt things deeply, and that was a good thing, an attribute to be proud of, though I didn't know how she could gauge my feelings, and I didn't believe heightened sensitivity was any kind of gift. The world of boyhood and of organized sports supported my theory. Sensitive became a swear word, one I avoided, hated. I hid mine, or tried to, tried not to take everything personally, which I did anyway.

In that sense, fishing offered a kind of reprieve from a world that often overwhelmed me. The fish didn't care about my disposition, and they lived by instincts invisible to me, feeding in the morning and evening as I did and, like me, operated at the disposal of weather systems, seasons. They didn't care about my presence, unless I hooked one, and I was comforted by their indifference, as I was comforted by the ways the seasons clicked on without consultation. I loved the beauty of the Serpentine and the other waters I fished and loved returning to them in my own various seasons of mind.

I fished in thunderstorms, blizzards, heat waves. I remember long fishless periods. Punctuating those long droughts and dips of frustration were moments of pure exhilaration, moments that seemed to reset and realign me—a boil appearing where my Rapala had been, my drag whining as a largemouth darted for cover or leapt and broke the stillness of evening. I loved coming in with a story to share.

My friends went to pit parties. They held New Year's Eve gatherings, drank beer like any bored, rural high school kids do. Meanwhile, I went to bed by nine so I could wake up before light to fish. I preferred fly rods to joints, tying flies to watching after-school fistfights. "Where's Brody?" I imagined my friends asking. "Oh, probably fishing," someone else adds. I never developed a taste for speed, jacked up trucks, or country music, despite their popularity within my peer groups. I liked girls, more so by the day in fact, and brought a few fishing, though it always ended up feeling like a production I didn't want to be part of. I preferred to fish alone, or with those who appreciated fishing just as much—or more so—than I did.

My father, Steven, was one of those people. He grew up fishing for bass and hunting whitetails with friends in New York state. He moved to Maine with my mother, Madeleine, Brooklyn-born, not an angler by any means, in 1977. He earned his Master Maine Guide's license before I was born and took clients striper fishing on the lower Kennebec River until he lost his ability to tolerate their bullshit. He was content to fish with his son, and I wanted to fish all the time. It was he who introduced me to fly fishing when I was ten; he had been introduced by a friend back in New York, since his father was often gone on work trips, and they rarely fished together. I wonder now if, by fishing with me so often, he was making up for lost time.

We spent summer evenings on the Kennebec, in Solon, him pointing out rises and me casting my not-so-pretty loops at the faint rings, brown trout, some big enough to break my leader. That a large and wary trout would eat feathers floating on a tiny hook baffled and exhilarated me. I couldn't get enough.

Even after Dad's heart issues, which were numerous and scary to witness, we went fishing together. During my parent's prolonged separation and after their eventual divorce, we went fishing together.

We didn't talk much on the water, and when we did it was mostly about the fishing itself: which fly to choose, or where to cast and when, exactly, we should quit. I always wanted a few more casts and Dad, I'm sure, wanted to get home before midnight. I'm not sure if we were avoiding harder conversations, or just caught up in the moment. My father was a counselor by trade, talked to people for a living, so it's not that he was particularly laconic, or that he didn't have experience talking about difficult topics.

I struggled to make sense of my parent's split. Neither parent had a clear explanation for their fracture, just that they had drifted apart over the years. They continued to co-parent Emily and me. They came to all our games and events, and they seemed to get along better as friends. Most of my friends' parents were married and there was no playbook for navigating a broken family as a twelve-year-old, even though I knew divorce was not uncommon in the world at large. My father the therapist and my mother the high school teacher—surely they had experience dealing with conflict, and I fantasized that they would get back together, which of course they did not do. The lack of resolution, the lack of clarity, buried itself somewhere inside me. Moving water helped. A clear directive helped: an open evening and my five-weight and a waiting canoe and the river nearby.

More than once Dad and I spent long evenings in the canoe not talking at all, and me not knowing exactly why I felt irritated, or frustrated, or angry, or to whom my feelings should be directed.

Over the years, we grew closer as I dealt with some of that buried frustration, as I acknowledged and tried to accept myself, and my father, even as he remarried, divorced, and remarried again; as my mother remained, by choice, alone. Grandpa Al died, and Anne sold the camp on the Serpentine to an out-of-state couple who painted the exterior gray, and ripped out the rotting dock to build a new one.

Dad and I didn't and still don't always have deep conversations on the water but sometimes we do, and we often reminisce about memories we've made together. We fish and hunt together when we can, which is not as often as I'd like.

It's amazing how passion flares, catches, moves with startling speed—a wildfire jumping roads and ditches. I did not expect those hours with the red and white bobber to flash with such intensity, to catch and bloom beyond any expectation, to engulf so much of my time and energy and thought, the way that it has. I worry I've spent so much time on the water, have developed my angling muscle to such an extent that other parts of me have atrophied. I suppose that's true of any passion, and sometimes I worry mine will consume me, or restrict me from vital components of life, like building my own family, or living with some semblance of financial security.

As I've grown older, I've gravitated toward fishing that requires precision, patience, and resolve. I graduated from red and white bobber to floating Rapala, then to a fly rod. The first fish I caught on a fly was a stunted largemouth bass in a kettle pond near my house, in the early evening on a mouse fly, my father in the stern of the canoe. I loved the predation—the way the small bass leaped from the pond to grab the easy floating meal. Since that moment, I've sought a visual component as I trick fish with feathers. Even more failure, then, failure as a kind of expectation, a welcome guest on most outings, but me going anyway, experimenting, grinding, until something good happened.

The first time a tarpon ate my fly, oceanside near Lower Matecumbe Key, in Islamorada, Florida, some mechanism in my brain shifted, realigned—I'm not sure exactly what happened—and I haven't been the same since. My fly line clinched around a button on my shirt and the leader broke. The tarpon swam off, but I was soaring. I've fished for them every spring since. If I have the opportunity and good fortune, if I can parlay teaching and writing and fly-tying with some other feasible income, I'll fish for tarpon every year until I can no longer stand on the deck of a skiff. Tarpon electrify me, bring me to life, demand that I live attentively in the moment.

Tarpon, snook, muskellunge, carp—the toughest fish to fool with flies, that's how I spend my time. I can't explain it, not exactly, and I worry a clear explanation might rob me of the ineffable joys of the pursuit.

My father has always identified as a hunter first, angler second. For years I interrogated my own alignment and wondered why I was more in tune with angling, wondered if that meant I was *less* of a hunter, if I was, after all, too sensitive to partake in harvesting animals. It took me years to recognize my flawed thinking, how such compartmentalizing diminishes the complexity, and similarity, of our passions.

Which is all to say: like my father, I am first and foremost a hunter, even if much of my hunting is done with a fly rod, with feathers affixed to a hook. I love the other kinds of hunting, too, especially for whitetail and moose—the ritual and camaraderie, the precision and patience required, but mostly I dream of fins and waters.

Hunting begs reconnection with my senses, and a pushing back against sensory-deadening screen time. I can offer that hunting touches upon some primitive human mechanism, which is true but also feels beyond the limitations of words. For me, the act of hunting is the act of focus—attention, stillness, listening, reacting. It is the forum in which I feel most alive.

The French artist and director Agnès Varda famously said, "If we opened people up, we'd find landscapes." I understand what she meant. If you opened me up—as you might, to some degree, by reading this book—you'll find landscapes: pine forests and winding rivers of Aroostook County, Maine; shallow, white-washed expanses of frozen New England lakes; a brackish bog where I first learned to fish; turquoise flats of Florida Bay. I realize the oddity and messiness of linking Maine and Florida, polar opposites in many categories, two territories at the termini of Route 1, governed at each end of the spectrum, but somehow, they've become kindred, linked, at least to me.

If you opened me up, you might also find those I care about most, those I choose to spend time with outdoors, where I am my most myself. My father, of course, is in here often, as he must be; and my dear friend, Parker, who is like a little brother to me, one of the most kind-hearted humans I know, who still needs another ten feet on his goddamn fly cast; and my guide-turned-good-friend Rich, Rich with a similar fire, consumed in some sense by the same passion but navigating it, somehow, oscillating between indulgence and homeostasis.

Occasionally, as I dig back through years of accumulated gear, through discarded tackle boxes, I find an old red and white bobber. The plastic globe is dusty and weathered, cracked, an abandoned miniature planet. I cannot recycle it, will never use it again, unless I have children, which is, at this point, very much up in the air. I lift the bobber—barely any weight at all—and wonder where I would be without it.

I'm not concerned about hero photographs, or in filling some ego-need to pass on wisdom or accumulated knowledge. I am still fairly young in the scheme of things, not yet forty, have been alive a millisecond in comparison to the landscapes and waterways I return to. I'm still learning and will always learn something valuable every time I venture outdoors. What I'm aiming for, then, when I head to the woods and waters I love, is a story—some meaningful, specific moment, unknowable, unbelievable, until it happens; a narrative to archive and revisit, when I need a true story more than anything else.

Here are a few of those stories.

RISES

Late July and Upper Pierce Pond is empty. I'm fifteen or sixteen, and Dad and I are killing time until the evening hatch, that brief window when mayflies dry their wings on the surface and fish gorge themselves. It's only noon. We're trolling copper Mooselook Wobblers on lead core line, five colors down, probing the depths because the surface is warm, and the resident brook trout and landlocked salmon are holding to deep thermoclines. Even the loons are silent.

It's a guilty pleasure for Mainers like us, trolling trout ponds in the heat of summer, but it usually works, and I'm too young to care much about our method. The 4-horse Yamaha sputters and chokes. A breeze ruffles the pond but it's not enough to cool us—we're both sweating. We circle the basin twice, which takes forever at trolling speed. Nothing doing. We have a five-weight fly rod rigged with floating line and a caddis imitation, but it's just taking up space. We don't say much. We're waiting for something, anything, to happen. I'm seated facing backward, toward Dad, minding the rods, while Dad directs the outboard's tiller; we look past each other's gaze.

The longer we go without catching something, the smaller our 17-foot square-stern canoe feels, the more I feel the sun's heat. Mid-day doldrums, and I can feel my hopefulness draining.

We have fished enough together, Dad and I, have seen enough success in this same canoe, that long fishless spells like this one begin to frustrate me. I try to ignore my frustration as I watch green lead core line splice the surface. After all, Dad and I are here together, spending time in one of our favorite places, away from everything and everyone, at least for a few days, and that should be enough.

We've returned here every summer since I was twelve, staying first at Cobb's Camps, with its classic log cabins and 6 p.m. community dinners on the Lower Pond, and then branching off to the Upper Pond islands—$20 per night for primitive campsites, an entire island to ourselves. We make our own meals and set our own schedule, which revolves entirely around the fishing. We sleep in the same double tent, which is an adventure given Dad's snoring, and the way that snoring drives me nearly insane, and the blow-up air mattress deflating by the middle of the night, so that we have fill it again in the dark. Still, it's a yearly retreat we both look forward to.

Despite its remoteness, Pierce Pond is only an hour and a half north of home, not far from The Forks, where whitewater rafters flock each summer. The last ten or so miles are spent navigating logging roads from which loaded pulp trucks raise plumes of dust. A handful of years earlier, my father had let me drive the entrance road on our way into Cobb's Camps. I was twelve and drove slowly, carefully. I was listening to Dad's story about his caddying job: teenage years, New York state, where he grew up, him yelling "Left! LEFT!" and me thinking it was part of his story, him coaxing a golf ball in a certain direction— around a dogleg, perhaps—instead of directing me to steer the pickup. I planted us in the right-hand ditch. In my shock, I kept my foot on the gas pedal, despite Dad's pleas, burying the

Pierce Pond was one of the first places where Dad took me fly fishing.

passenger-side tires. We got towed out by a passerby who did not seem to buy Dad's story that he had been behind the wheel and drifted off, distracted by something or other. It was a few years before Dad let me drive the entry road again.

This year, Dad drove the whole way. We had packed our camping gear and cooler of food and solar powered radio into the truck, along with our fly rods and trusty forest green square-stern Old Town, which we launched from the unimproved landing on Upper Pond. No shoreline development, no camps or docks, no cell service, just a well-worn walking path between fir trees that ended at the pond's northwest corner. At the launch, moose tracks pock-marked the mud and loon calls echoed against surrounding mountains. A red-spotted leech undulated through the shallows; dense Maine woods leaned in from all sides. Mosquitoes whined in our ears. We paddled the short distance to our island and unloaded—Dad meticulous in his organization, in setting up a tarp over the picnic table despite no rain in the forecast, and me wanting to go fishing as soon as possible, haphazardly tossing my sleeping bag near the tent to make room in the canoe, setting up my fly rod before I unpacked anything else.

We're camping for two nights on Bruce's Island, hoping to witness the storied hexagenia hatch. The large mayflies emerge in the coolest hours, typically in early July, resting on the surface to dry their delicate wings. Despite their efforts, many don't make it to flight, since they're such easy targets for the fish below. Sometimes—if our timing is right, and if the weather doesn't disrupt the event—big trout and salmon lose their inhibition. It happens late, and it's quick: twenty, thirty minutes, tops. Then we're casting to faint slurps in the dark, trying to keep our Stimulators away from dive-bombing bats.

We troll through the basin once more, rods fixed in their aluminum holders, tips bent under the heavy weight of our lines. Dad suggests lunch and points the canoe toward our campsite. I could eat. It's not like we're catching anything. An afternoon nap sounds good too, since Dad kept me awake with his snoring. Even when I woke him, he rolled over and started right up again. He likes to give me a hard time when I'm grumpy in the mornings, which is often. I apply another round of sunscreen to my ears and nose.

Halfway back to Bruce's Island the breeze stops, as if a breaker switched off. I turn and face forward, careful not to tip us. Within moments Upper Pierce Pond is a glass tabletop reflecting cirrus clouds, blue sky. A hundred yards ahead, a fish rises, then another.

Dad kills the motor and we glide toward the rises. "*Now* we're cooking," he says.

I wind in our trolling lines as fast as possible, which does not feel fast enough, then grab the five-weight, fixed with a size ten olive Elk Hair Caddis. I stand, steady myself, and prepare to cast. This is how we always fish: one of us in front, usually me, taking casts, while the other steadies the canoe, paddles quietly, lines up the angle. It takes a second to get my sea-legs after so much sitting, and the canoe wobbles.

"Woahhh," Dad says, grabbing the gunwales. "I don't want to go swimming."

"I got it," I say. "Don't worry."

Caddisflies skitter everywhere. They swerve and spin like drunk boatmen, intoxicated by the stillness and hot sun. Their movements flit and hiccup as if filmed at low frame rate. They dance atop one hundred feet of water leaving tiny nervous wakes. *Them tent-winged jobbies,* old timers call them. I don't know the proper scientific name, or where they came from, just that their sudden appearance feels miraculous.

Now two, three, four salmon rising. Salmon because they cover distance between rises, salmon because of their rise patterns: snout, dorsal, tail. The caddisflies don't stand a chance.

We get in range.

"Take your time," Dad says. I lay out a long cast, twitch my fly to life. "Good."

Silence. My fly is a miniature island. I wonder if the canoe has overtaken the fish, or if the salmon hasn't seen my presentation. Then my fly disappears beneath a closing snout. After the set, the salmon sprints, somersaults, then dives for the thermocline.

Dad nets it a few minutes later. "Beauty," he says.

I wet my hands, then remove my fly from the corner of the salmon's mouth. I revive it gently, three pounds of silver in my hands: gone.

The weather report on the radio calls for evening thunderstorms, which could wash out the evening hatch, but for now I couldn't care less. The canoe feels spacious and welcoming, the world aligned again—Dad and me, working in tandem, my hands smelling like salmon, the rough edges of tiredness smoothed over, at least for a little while.

What I don't know—can't know, in this moment—is that two days later, returning home from our camping trip, my father will suffer a heart attack on his bike ride, will see a white light then wake in a hospital bed, in Waterville, the town where I was born. I can't know that he will survive the close call, that we'll return to Upper Pierce Pond together, chasing rises in the middle of summer afternoons like this one.

A pond that five minutes ago seemed barren is now alive, salmon carving the still surface—missing caddisflies, not missing the second time—their rings expanding, dissipating, like some lost memory. I dry my fly. Dad paddles toward another rise.

"You sure you don't want to take a cast?"

"No way," he says. "Get ready. There's more fish rising."

I coil line on the floor of our canoe, hoping for another shot before the wind picks up.

NOVEMBER LIGHT

In an abandoned woodlot, three of us stumble through the late September morning, adrenaline overtaking our weariness. Two bull moose spar on a distant ridge. We approach them cautiously, single file: Shawn, my father's neighbor, hunting partner, and recruited moose-caller; my dad, Steven, seventy, faithful sub-permittee, struggling to keep up on bad knees; and me, twenty-nine, the Bull-Only permit holder. Dad has postponed knee replacement surgery until mid-winter, so he won't miss hunting season. Of the three of us, I am by far the least-accomplished hunter, which is at once comforting—the feeling one gets in the presence of experts—and, because of my historical bad luck and general lack of experience, a little intimidating. We're more than three hundred miles north of my Portland apartment, on the eastern perimeter of the Allagash Wilderness Waterway, with all its rivers, ponds, lakes, and forests, crisscrossed by logging roads and cuttings in various stages of regrowth. It's the second day of Maine's annual moose hunt.

Shawn stops and crouches beside an old logging road, among tangled alders a few feet ahead of me, trying to blend in. In his mid-forties, Shawn appears younger, blonde hair winged from beneath his camouflage baseball cap. With both hands cupped over his nose and mouth, he lets out a wailing call, opening his hands slightly and lifting his head to mimic an eager cow. His call sounds to me like a whiny child. Dad crowds in behind me, looks frazzled after another night sleeping on the ground. I'm a little worried about his health, given his heart issues and given our remoteness—I'd rather get a moose sooner than later, so his body isn't too taxed.

"They're both shooters," he whispers, his eyes on the bulls as he fingers his leather gun sling.

Two hundred yards away, in a clear-cut atop a ridgeline, the larger of the two sparring bulls turns to the sound of Shawn's call—apparently more intrigued by the prospect of female companionship than by fighting rivals—and lumbers toward us at full trot.

You've got to be kidding me, I think, dropping to a knee and opening my shooting bipod with a loud, unintended *clack*. Shawn repositions behind me, my father beside him. I rest my rifle on the bipod and thumb the safety. Through my scope, set to the fourth power of magnification, the moose's black body—crowned by magnificent, almond-colored antlers—appears too large to be real. It slows to a walk, having cut the distance between us in half. The moose stops and laps its tongue against its wide nose. The breeze is behind us, and I'm nervous as hell.

"I've got a shot," I whisper. My heart pounds.

"Wait—too far," Shawn whispers from over my shoulder. "Let him get closer."

A moment later, the bull steps from the logging road into the alder bushes, disappearing from my scope, from our view. I keep my scope fixed on the general area, waiting for the moose to reappear. Shawn makes another cow call. Nothing. I wait a few more seconds, then stand, collapse the bipod, and shoulder my rifle.

"I wonder what happened?" Shawn asks, though none of us has an answer. Dad steps out from the brush, perplexed.

"Must have winded us," he says.

On the basement wall of my childhood home, my father displayed the rack of every whitetail buck he'd ever shot. Many of the antlers were small: spikehorns, or four-pointers, screwed through small segments of skull to a horizontal wooden slab.

"The antlers have been a way for me to visually mark the passage of time and my own life," he told me once. Dad shot his first buck at age fourteen, on a hunting trip with his father, though he was alone when he killed the animal. "I kept thinking of how proud my father would be, and I dragged the deer a mile back to camp to meet him." It was a small buck, its antlers just a few inches, and his father couldn't hide his disappointment. My father felt rejected, confused. "Hunting has been a lifelong search for redemption, of sorts," he said. Looking at the wall of antlers, it was clear to me redemption for my father did not mean harvesting big bucks, but rather taking part in the yearly tradition of hunting, in the specificities of each hunt, and maybe proving to himself that he was a competent and thoughtful hunter.

Later in his teen years, my father harvested a big ten-pointer, hunting alone this time. After it dropped, he walked to the buck and lifted its enormous rack, then realized, with apprehension, he'd have to drag it out of the woods alone. For reasons unknown even to him, he named that deer Harold. The neck mount of Harold—some fifteen years older than me—had its spot on the same basement wall, set aside from the smaller, less impressive racks. When I was little, seven or eight years old, I stood below Harold and stared up at his marble, taxidermied eyes, and ran a finger over the glossy nose, removing accumulated dust. I found nothing spooky or morbid about Harold, or Dad's wall of antlers. They were my father's accomplishments—important enough to display, each rack containing stories he liked to retell—and I felt nearer to him, and proud, standing there.

When I was ten, Dad took me hunting for the first time. I sat in silence beside him in a two-man metal tree stand. My butt sank into the camouflaged cushion on the bench seat that supported us. The November sun was still below the horizon, but there was enough light to see. From the stand, we faced a narrow valley, at the bottom of which a small stream gurgled over mossy rocks. The far bank rose sharply, then leveled off into a stand of white birch. This was posted property, but my father had secured access from the local dairy farmer who owned it; I could hear the occasional bellow of the farmer's cows in the field a hundred yards behind us. Under the safety-conscious eye of my father, I had graduated from pellet gun to .22 to .410 shotgun, to the short-stocked .243 rifle that rested in my lap. We were hunting whitetail. The morning was windless.

To our left a twig snapped and my head swung to the sound. My heartbeat quickened. A few seconds passed. From the undergrowth, a fat squirrel hopped through fallen leaves. Dad leaned to my ear and whispered: "If you have to move, move slowly." I nodded. I didn't know how long I could keep still.

Ten or fifteen minutes later, Dad elbowed my shoulder. Through the trees to our left, a patch of brown. A deer stepped from behind a tree, its ears pricked, then stopped, frozen. It was forty yards away. How did it get so close without making a sound? The deer stepped forward and turned to us, flicked its tail, stopped again, eyes fixed on our stand. There was empty space between its ears—a doe.

She watched me for what felt like several minutes, her neck a white bib of hair. She dropped her head and began to browse on the forest floor, meandering up the ridge toward our stand. I lifted my rifle, disengaged the safety, then peered through my scope. I watched her eat, now twenty yards away. She chewed, then turned her head to a sound I could not hear and froze, then relaxed and chewed again. With the scope's magnification, I could see the doe's long black eyelashes. It was as though I forgot I was hunting, forgot that I had secured a doe permit, so transfixed was I in the excitement of watching. I did not shoot.

When the doe eased into the cedar thicket to our right, having spent a half hour feeding near our stand, my father patted my shoulder.

"She was beautiful, wasn't she?" he whispered. He was smiling. "That was a big doe. Great practice for you to look at her through the scope." I was relieved I had not disappointed him by letting her walk.

Shortly after I turned twelve, my parents separated. They made the announcement to my sister, Emily, and me at the dinner table one evening. Dad moved into an old one-room schoolhouse on our property, before moving in with another woman, and eventually remarrying. He suffered several heart attacks over the next handful of years, events his doctors struggled to understand: he was a non-smoker, an active outdoorsman, an ex-football player, never overweight, never sedentary. He underwent successful bypass surgery and would need a second bypass years later. In the confusing aftermath of the divorce and his health issues, I didn't spend any less time with him. We fly-fished together dozens of times each summer, duck and deer hunted each fall. But I was angry and hurt and confused by his departure, and fearful of a more permanent one.

I was unsure of where to direct the feelings, and Dad often took the brunt.

When I outgrew the two-man stand, we hunted from separate tree stands. I would see does—many of them, it seemed—but never bucks. I wanted my first deer to be a buck, a good one, so I stopped applying for doe permits. Dad shot a nice buck every season, it seemed.

"I put in the time," he'd say, whenever I complained about my luck.

And he was right: he hunted three or four days a week, continued to rise morning after morning, hours before the sun, to get in position before shooting light. As my unsuccessful deer seasons piled up, I felt an internal pressure mounting. Still, I was happy to participate in the ritual, in an activity my father considered sacred: 4 a.m. alarm clock, bleary-eyed breakfasts, walking behind Dad through dark woods, navigating with the faint beam of our headlamps, stars still bright above us. Dad was careful with his steps and went to great efforts to avoid snapping twigs or crunching leaves that might alert the deer of our approach. There was something primitive about those mornings—how many thousands of years, I wondered, had fathers and sons gone hunting together? I liked watching the woods wake up; I found comfort in the plans we made to part and meet back up again at an agreed upon time. I wondered what he was seeing from his stand, and I waited to hear the crack of his rifle. But by the end of November, having failed again to fill my tag, I would feel familiar disappointment; I was participating, spending valuable time with my father outdoors, sharing in the activity he loved most, but I was not contributing meat to the freezer, or racks for his wall. Maybe I was not cut out for it.

In Maine, a first-time moose permit applicant has about an eight percent chance of being drawn. My grandfather, Andrew (my middle name), aka Al, applied for a Maine moose tag twenty straight years without being selected—he died with a Maine moose hunt on his bucket list. So, when I scrolled through the lottery results on my father's laptop, at his home in Industry around Father's Day, a few months after my twenty-ninth birthday, I was stunned to see my name. I re-read it to myself a few times before saying anything aloud. Brod, Ryan, Bull Only, Zone 2, September season. My father overheard from the couch where he was watching the Red Sox, and he stood up and shouted his congratulations.

I knew that this zone, which creates the eastern boundary of the Allagash wilderness, contains a high-density moose population—more moose than people. The rolling hills are spliced by logging roads, controlled by the North Maine Woods, and the cuttings bring new growth that attracts browsing moose. Of the three months in the moose hunting season (September through November), September is often best, given the proximity to the rut. The bulls have one thing on their minds, so they respond well to calls. My father was ecstatic; it's the same zone he'd drawn the year before, when he killed a beautiful eight-hundred-pound bull. He had called me from his truck a few hours after shooting his bull that previous October. I was with my then-girlfriend in a Subway in rural South Dakota, during a cross-country road trip. We'd planned our trip before his name was drawn—and I felt as though I'd missed out on a once-in-a-lifetime hunt. My permit felt like redemption.

But the biggest animal I had shot to date was a turkey; I had yet to kill a deer, a streak that had lasted nearly twenty years. When I heard an approaching deer in the woods, my pulse raced, and my palms sweated. It felt as though the deer—hyper-aware of its surroundings—could sense my own nervousness, which acted as deer repellant. Part of the nerves, I imagined, came from a lack of confidence in shooting. Some years I didn't practice shooting at all.

So in early July, two months before my moose hunt, I brought my Ruger .308, two cases of shells, and a large paper target to Shawn's cornfield, in New Sharon, and spent the afternoon shooting. I brought a newly purchased bipod—a small, inexpensive device that would help hold my gun steady. I practiced thumbing the safety, pushing it forward gently to avoid any noise. I practiced holding the crosshairs over the target for several seconds, imagining a bull moose standing broadside. I practiced exhaling slowly before pulling the trigger. I rushed a couple of bad shots. A few minutes later, I hit the bullseye. A week later, back in the same field, I chambered a shell, set the bipod in the tall grass, and lowered the crosshairs to the target. I pushed the safety, my extended finger touching the cold trigger. I exhaled and squeezed. I shot the entire box of shells. Over and over, I hit the target's center. The repetition, the firing on my own time—and the slow breathing—all contributed to a newfound sense of control, and confidence.

Dad and I leave for the North Maine Woods at daybreak, three days prior to the September moose season. So far, the weather has been a continuation of summer; we lower the windows to flush out swarming mosquitoes.

His truck, and the trailer behind us, is stuffed with tents, sleeping bags, cooking utensils, coolers of food and drink, camouflage rain gear, rope, and pulleys. As my chosen sub-permittee, Dad is legally able to shoot, so long as he's within sight of me. Our plan is that he'll follow up my initial shot only if the moose is still standing. Our .308 rifles—my bolt-action

Ruger, and his Remington lever—are cased in hard black plastic, side by side in the back seat.

Shawn trails behind in his beat-up Subaru. A skilled welder, he's taken three days off to join us. He has hunted with my father since he was a teenager, a connection made by my mother, who was his high school teacher. Stricken with severe claustrophobia, Shawn cannot tolerate a night in a tent without ripping his way out, so his Subaru doubles as transportation and—with seat dropped back and windows open—sleeping quarters. A sought-after welder and accomplished deer hunter, Shawn is a marvel at spotting far-off game through impossibly thick cover. He hunts with open sights and kills deer at distances that would warrant congratulations to a scoped hunter. He's also a fantastic caller of turkeys and moose, a master tracker, and handyman. He is woods-smart and resourceful; the kind of guy you want along with you on a moose hunt in the Maine wilderness. He has two sons, but neither has showed interest in hunting.

Half an hour into our drive, Dad, from behind the wheel of his Silverado says, "I've got a few things we need to talk about, some of which are a little bit heavy."

Historically, we aren't very good at this kind of thing, and I'm hoping we can get it over with quickly and enjoy the rest of the ride.

"OK," I say.

"The doctor found a blip on my latest scan," he says, matter-of-factly. "Seems that the artery they replaced in my second bypass is getting blocked up again."

We both stare straight ahead. I take a deep breath. I've learned to live with a constant, often dormant anxiety, a persistent fear that my father will drop dead.

"Protocol," he continues, "is that they won't do anything invasive until I have symptoms. Which, as you know, I've never had before any of my six heart attacks."

"So what does that mean for you?" I ask. We merge onto the highway in Pittsfield.

"Well, nothing really," Dad says. "I'll keep doing what I'm doing. I feel fine. I just wanted you to be aware of what was going on."

"I guess that's a good thing, then, that you're feeling fine." I wipe my eyes with my sleeve. I wonder what the passing drivers must think, two grown men in camo, towing a trailer up I-95 North, crying and sniffling. "Thanks for letting me know," I say. "Can we talk about something else now?"

Dad chuckles. He reaches over and puts his hand on my shoulder and squeezes. "In other news, are you ready for that big bull moose?"

Shawn and Dad are discussing our next move when a bull appears suddenly, the same bull as before, I realize, at a head-on angle in the center of the logging road from which it had disappeared.

What happens next is a blur: I drop again to one knee, unfold the bipod, rest the rifle stock, disarm the safety. Through the scope I watch the bull take two steps forward, never taking his eyes from me. I drop the crosshair to a point on its lower chest. I finger the trigger and squeeze.

My father fires. The successive concussions rattle in my ears. The bull does not flinch, gives no obvious sign of being hit. It simply saunters into the alders, as if he's seen just enough of the three strange creatures in camouflage.

"Shit," Shawn says.

"You think you hit it?" Dad asks.

"I think so—crosshairs were right on him. What about you?" Dad shakes his head, shrugs. "My scope was fogged up . . . I don't know."

"Let's give it a while and then look for blood," Shawn says.

I replay the shot over and over in my mind. *I must have hit it,* I think to myself. How could I miss a target as massive as a moose? More than the idea of missing, I hate to think about wounding such an animal, and not finding it.

We wait about twenty minutes, then the three of us walk to where we believe the moose was standing when we fired. We have trouble finding tracks. There is no blood, no hair. I am doubting myself. I am embarrassed. I walk farther down the road, leaving Shawn and Dad behind.

From ahead I hear a raspy, complicated exhale, slow and labored. Then a long silence. I step cautiously in the grass that has grown like a mohawk down the logging road's center. I lift my rifle closer to my chest. I wonder if I am hearing things, or if I'd heard my own breathing. But then I hear the noise again, closer. A single exhale, slower, more gravelly than before. Then nothing.

I take a few more steps forward, crouched, and ready. I thumb the safety. In my periphery, I catch brownish red against a background of greens and yellows. I turn and my eyes focus on jagged tines of a palmated antler, extending upward amongst tall grass and a cluster of white wildflowers. I feel as though in a dream.

With the safety off I step cautiously the fifteen feet from logging road to the rear end of the moose. I expect the bull to jump and disappear into the thick cover it was headed for when it fell. I half expect the giant creature, sprawled on its side in the weeds, to vanish entirely. At a gun's length, I nudge the muzzle against the moose's hind leg. I watch the massive black chest for movement. Nothing.

At some point I yell back to Dad and Shawn, who are some fifty yards behind. I rest my rifle against a nearby tree and then kneel in the space between the bull's front and hind legs.

Its coat is a dew-slicked charcoal. It steams. A small tuft of silver guard hair spikes from the very top of its hump. I run my hand over its barrel chest. The moose smells sweetly of cedar and bog and earth. The scent is strong; I wonder how long it will last. The eye facing up is open and clear. There is a fleck of lung—pink, spongey—stuck to the moose's neck. I feel no guilt for killing the moose—instead, a sense of awe at its size and beauty, and a deep reverence for the animal.

My father and Shawn catch up. There are high fives, hugs, and tears. We take to field dressing the animal, and after my first few incisions, I'm alarmed at the amount of blood that pools out onto the ground. It's more than the earth can absorb. The moose's chest cavity is so large, after I've cleared out the entrails, that I must bury my arm to the shoulder in the moose's ribcage—my head resting against its ribs—to remove its vital organs: lungs, liver, heart.

There is a Native ritual, my Dad tells me, as we're dressing the moose, in which a hunter who has taken his first animal has that animal's blood smeared on his cheeks by an elder. It's a right-of-passage kind of thing. I'm not sure if this is historically accurate, or if it's something Dad's heard and retained, somewhere in the annals of his fading memory, recalibrating the story to his own liking, to this scene. It makes me self-conscious to think about, but then I remember there is no one else around, except Shawn. Dad runs his pointer finger inside the breached chest cavity, then streaks blood along my cheeks.

Dad calls a week or so after the moose hunt. We've paid a friend to quarter and refrigerate the moose until we can set aside a weekend to butcher it ourselves. It will take the three of us—Dad, Shawn, and me—the better part of two days to deconstruct the moose and fill our freezers with vacuum-sealed packs of violet-colored meat. We will end up buying a new freezer to fit it all.

"You sure you didn't hit it?" I ask Dad.

He concedes that his shot was errant—he could barely see out of his fogged-up scope. "I'm sure. That was your shot that dropped him, positive. I wasn't surprised you made that shot when you needed to."

He tells me he's printed photos of me field dressing the moose, where it had fallen among wildflowers and changing leaves. My hands and arms are slicked with blood. In one of the photos, he says, I'm holding up the moose's heart, which is as big as a cantaloupe. I'm cradling it, delicately, holding it up so the camera can capture the small, single bullet hole that brought the moose down.

A few months after the hunt, Dad gifts me a maple burl—curly maple, he calls it—onto which the moose head is mounted. It's a European-style mount, just skull and antlers. Sutures spike and dip along the skull like EKG waves. The empty eye sockets could hold golf balls. He and Shawn have signed the back of the burl in black sharpie, with the date and location of the hunt. I sign my name next to theirs. The antler spread is the width of my outstretched arms. I'll find a place for it on the walls on my apartment.

In November, I spend three days in a tree stand at one of Dad's favorite haunts. It's the middle of rifle season, and the deer should be moving. Still, I don't see much, aside from squirrels, and one yearling doe that walks by at dark on the third evening, quiet and ghostly. I think of the doe I let pass that first day, decades ago, and wonder what might be different now had I pulled the trigger.

Three days later and I'm back home in my Portland apartment, an hour-and-a-half drive south of Dad's. He calls me at 8:30 a.m. on one of my days off.

"Well," he says, "I'm gonna need a little help."

He doesn't have to explain himself. "Please don't drag it yourself," I say. He's done it before, and it worries me. Dragging a buck puts a lot of strain on his heart.

"That's why I called you!" he says, and I can tell he's smiling. "Shawn's going to meet you up by the road."

"I'm on my way."

I drive north on I-95 to help Dad haul his buck from the woods. He had been sitting in the same stand I'd worn out over the past few days.

Shawn is parked near Dad's truck when I arrive.

"Figured I'd wait for you before I walked down to meet him," Shawn says. Even though Dad had told me he'd be there, Shawn's gesture surprises me. I take it as a sign of respect, as if to say, I defer to you, the hunter's son, in this moment.

We find Dad standing near his weather-beaten ladder stand, with its chipping camoflauge paint job, at the edge of a bog, in a swath of late-morning sunlight. His .308 leans against a fir tree. A mature eight-point buck lies at his feet, already field dressed. Its rack is medium-sized, symmetrical, with tines the color of honey.

Dad hugs me, then Shawn. I haven't seen him this excited in a while, not since the moose hunt.

"So around eight, I got out my thermos," Dad says, happy finally for the captive audience. "Figured it was all over by then, I hadn't seen shit and the sun was getting high, you know? I finished my hot chocolate and screwed the lid back on the thermos, but then I dropped it. CLANK! Right against the side of my ladder. Next thing I know, this buck jumped out from behind

My dad's wife, Pamela, friend Shawn, and Dad moose hunting.

me—he must have snuck in because I never heard him. Stood broadside at forty feet. I touched one off and down he went."

"Unbelievable," Shawn says.

Unbelievable, I think. I'm proud of him. We take photos.

Shawn and I drag the buck the short distance to the edge of the field. Dad walks up ahead of us, finding the best path, stopping to look back and checking our progress. His elbows chicken-wing behind him. He looks like an old man. It's amazing how easily the buck slides over leaves, downed branches, a stone wall. Once we reach the field, Dad gets his truck and backs it up, and Shawn and I lift the animal onto the waiting bed. I'm content for the moment to participate, to share in Dad's excitement. Shawn and I crouch in the bed with the deer between us, Dad driving us slowly through the open field, back to where we've parked our cars. The sky is clear in its autumnal way, November light angled and sharp.

What is it we want from our fathers? Not to become them, not to reject them. I don't have the answer. A writing mentor told me, having read my work—*You know, we are here essentially to replace our parents.* I had never thought of it that way before.

Crouching in the back of Dad's pick-up, my right hand holds the buck's antlers to steady myself against the bumps—divots in the field, rocks pushing up through the earth. Hunting season is almost over. Between my moose and Dad's deer, we'll have plenty of meat for the long winter.

There is no guarantee, but I sense my father and I will have more hunts together: whitetail, and turkey, and even moose, if we're lucky again in the lottery. It occurs to me, as Dad slows his truck at our parked cars so Shawn and I can hop out, that what we're aiming for is not a kill, or a set of antlers for the wall, but a story. A story to tell one another, and retell again later, rich with details seared into our memory: a doe's delicate eyelashes, the sweet stink of a moose, the clank of a thermos against a ladder stand. And when our hunting stories conclude with a harvest—as they rarely do—the kill itself cannot be shared. Each rack on Dad's wall, the moose skull soon to be on mine—they hold their own stories, but the taking of each animal is personal, a private, numinous event.

I hope I am with him, as witness, when he leaves these woods for good.

TEN-YEAR TARPON

'm in the backcountry of Florida Bay, somewhere between Islamorada and Flamingo, gripping the cork handle of a Hardy 11-weight fly rod. Pinched between my left thumb and pointer finger is a custom-tied tarpon fly with lime-green eyes and chicken-feather tail. The Hell's Bay skiff under my bare feet drafts seven inches and costs more than most SUVs. From my vantage point on the casting platform, I can't see Rich—my sandy-haired, twenty-something guide—but I know he's back there. Every few seconds, I hear the muffled crunch of his push pole biting through the turtle grass. The skiff glides over shallow-water flats as adroitly as a water snake.

Silhouettes of small mangrove islands complicate the horizon. In the foreground, a cormorant rests atop a wooden channel marker, wings spread, facing the sunrise. The bay's surface is a mirror; it will be a few hours before the sun is high enough for optimal sight fishing.

It's the middle of March and I'm pale from a long Maine winter. Ever susceptible to sunburn, I've taken sun protection to the extreme: Beige sun pants, long-sleeve paneled sun shirt, bonefish-patterned breathable sun mask snugly over my mouth and nose, and hat. I resemble an overdressed tropical bank robber.

I've been looking forward to this day with the kind of anticipation that makes sleep difficult. Events of the past 24 hours—digging my car out from under a Maine snowstorm, cramming into the middle seat of a 737, mind-numbing inertia of traffic jams on Route 1 South, squishing cockroaches in the bathroom of my shitty motel room—seem worth the hassle. It also seems reasonable that I'm paying Rich, an accomplished angler and up-and-coming tarpon guide, what amounts to one month's rent for his services. I'm here to finally land a tarpon with a fly rod.

The sun, higher now, begins to light up the flats. The contrast of cloudless blue sky against light green water is stunning—I've grown accustomed to muted, monochrome whites and grays of New England winter. We're in a spot Rich calls Pelican Lake, a wide basin with soft turtle-grass bottom where early-season tarpon congregate. There are small mangrove islands in all directions, and the air is a mix of tidal smells: salt, sulfur, and something sweeter I can't identify. Rich is surprised we're the only boat around. I'm glad to be far from downtown Islamorada, with its bustling tourist shops, its traffic and strip malls.

Rich calls out from his poling platform above the white Suzuki outboard: "Okay, Ryan. There's a big single coming in, ten o'clock."

"I don't see it."

"Look farther out," Rich says. "It's pushing a wake. *Trust me,* you'll see it."

A hundred feet away, the tarpon's wake is the vertex of an intimidating V. The fish is swimming directly toward our bow. I imagine this is what an incoming torpedo might look like.

"I see it now, Rich."

"Wait for it to get closer," he says, his voice lower now. "Remember, they're spooky when it's this calm. No unnecessary movements. I'll tell you when to cast."

The big tarpon—a female, recognizable due to its immense size—flicks its powerful tail against the dropping tide. Rich gives the command to cast, and I land the fly four feet ahead of the tarpon. With my left hand I strip line, bringing the fly to life. The tarpon takes notice of the fly, which I'm trying to sell as a fleeing baitfish.

"Come on, eat it," Rich whispers. "She's gonna eat it."

I keep stripping and anticipate the strike. The fish follows for several feet, its mouth inches behind my fly. Thirty feet from the boat, the tarpon flushes wildly. My fly boils to the surface in the tarpon's tail-wash.

"What the hell?" Rich says. He lets out a loud, irritated sigh. "Everything looked perfect. Something must have spooked her. Check that fly."

The fly's tail feathers are not fouled, and the 50-pound fluorocarbon leader is clean. Rich continues poling for a few minutes, then says, "That was a big girl."

Over the next hour, my poor casting spooks dozens of approaching tarpon. The fish arrive in pairs, strings, and swimming wedges. The hyper-clear water doesn't help; it offers visual confirmation of the tarpon's various reactions to my fly, ranging from mildly perturbed to downright fearful. It's as though my fly is tarpon repellant. I'm rattled. Pelican Lake has eaten me up.

"You've gotta let it go, man. I can tell you're flustered," Rich says, after I've blown another shot. "*They* can tell you're flustered. Just forget about it. You'll get plenty more shots today."

My passion for tarpon fishing, and my dream-turned-obsession of landing one with a fly rod, had been set in motion ten years earlier when my father treated me to an unexpected college graduation present: he said he'd take me fishing anywhere in the U.S., for any species I wanted to catch. Without much hesitation, I chose tarpon fishing in the Florida Keys. I had been introduced to tarpon by Saturday morning outdoor television—*Walker's Cay Chronicles* and *Spanish Fly*—and it was easy for a young Maine angler, accustomed to wild but tiny brook trout, to become seduced by the tarpon's size and power.

On that trip, our first morning in Islamorada, my father and I watched a tarpon rocket out of Florida Bay, the first we'd ever seen in person. It looked too big, too powerful to be real. If you've never seen a tarpon, imagine a six-foot, silver-plated prehistoric fish with oversized eyes and an underbite that jumps and thrashes when hooked, trying wildly to throw your hook and often succeeding, what with its bony mouth and penchant for impressive aerobatics. After that first fish fell back to the water, and the angler fighting it from the stern of a guide's boat hollered with excitement, I made two observations. First: the saltwater spinning gear my father and I had prepared for this, our first Keys tarpon trip, was too flimsy to catch something like *that*. Second: we had no idea what we were doing. These realizations didn't stop us from trying.

We fished from a leaky rental boat, using dead mullet—the bait that locals recommended—in deep channels near the Overseas Highway. The heat was oppressive, the sun inescapable. We reminded each other to hydrate every few hours. Guide skiffs whizzed by our anchored clunker, amplifying our feeling that they were on to something we didn't yet understand. The few tarpon we did see were swimming fast and showed no interest in eating our offerings.

On the afternoon of day four, thirty minutes before the rental boat was due back, a fish took one of our baits and pulled out a hundred yards of line without jumping. I fought it for fifteen minutes, at which point my fantasy of landing a tarpon was deflated by the brown, tadpole shape of a docile nurse shark, its body undulating like an eel. I cut the line.

The next spring, we returned to Islamorada, having booked a local guide named Bruce. When we met Bruce at the dock, he was carrying two oversize spinning rods in one hand and a package of frozen mullet in the other. Bruce was pot-bellied, wore his hair in a ponytail, and walked with a noticeable limp. Dad told him, as we loaded into his center console, that we'd had no luck with mullet the previous spring. I explained to Bruce that we were both fishing guides back in Maine and wanted desperately to learn how to catch tarpon.

"Okay," Bruce said. "You *really* want to catch a tarpon? Meet me back here at 7 p.m."

That evening we drifted live crabs on an incoming tide. After a quiet first hour, about when the doubt crept in, Dad, from the front of Bruce's boat, muttered under his breath and lifted his rod. A massive, head-shaking tarpon, airborne for a brief moment at the end of his line and making a sound—a distinct rattling of gills and cartilage. Dad never set the hook, and the fish was gone, but the sound that tarpon made remains with me.

A few seconds later, another tarpon ate my crab, swam to the boat, hurdled the raised outboard, peeling line at an alarming rate. Then slack. When I reeled in, the reinforced 8/0 J-hook (a size commonly used for marlin) was straightened. I was transfixed.

"That wasn't even a *big* one," Bruce had said. We jumped eight tarpon that night, Dad landing our first—a seventy-pounder—under a full moon.

I regret pulling that first tarpon from the water, draping it across our knees for a photograph. A fish that heavy isn't designed to be lifted out of the water by its head. I regret removing a palm-sized scale as a souvenir, too, but I needed proof. After snapping the photo, Bruce shifted the boat from forward to neutral and back, while I held the tired tarpon boatside by its lower jaw. Warm salt water rushed through the open bucket-mouth and over the fish's gills. I felt it strengthen. When I released my grip, the tarpon swam away under its own power.

Back at the dock, we thanked Bruce emphatically. He told us to come back and fish with him again, though we never did. He had taught us that tarpon feed best at night, and that live crabs are effective and easy to use. We'd learned enough from him to tarpon fish on our own.

Driving back to the hotel at midnight, exhilarated, thanking my father over and over, I set a new goal: catch a tarpon on a fly rod.

Rich is from New Hampshire. Despite being five years my junior, we might pass for the same age, his face and hands sun-worn. Like a lot of guides I've met, Rich was a high school athlete (baseball). He is short and compact, and it's easy to imagine him calling out directions to teammates from his position at shortstop.

Rich poles us to deeper water so he can lower the outboard and make a move. He is always poling, and prides himself on covering water, on hunting the shallow flats actively, rather than anchoring or staking out as other guides often do. I tell him how I'd spent hours at my tying bench, mimicking famous tarpon fly patterns: the Cockroach, the White Lightning, the Tarpon Toad, and later, invented my own.

For the 358 days a year I am not in Islamorada, I am a voracious consumer of all things tarpon. I read and re-read Thomas McGuane's *The Longest Silence* collection, study the history of fly fishing for tarpon in the Keys, devour less literary how-to books by guides who've spent their lives chasing the silver king. One off-season, I hired a fly-casting instructor for multiple sessions. In winter, I pretend I'm on the bow of a skiff and cast to sticks placed in the snow at various angles. Often, while lying in bed awaiting sleep, I visualize making the perfect cast to an oncoming tarpon. The fish eats my fly every time.

At our second stop, we find no fish. Rich jabs the push pole into the bottom, ropes it off to a cleat, and we break for lunch. I tell him the story of my first (and only) solo attempt to navigate the backcountry by rental boat the year before. I was tired of refusals from migratory oceanside tarpon, and it was common knowledge that backcountry fish were often more inclined to eat a well-placed fly. I figured an onboard GPS system and waterproof map were all I'd need to navigate the backcountry's winding channels and skinny-water flats.

"This story is not going to end well, is it?" Rich asks, scanning the water while he eats his sandwich.

I tell him that after several miles I noticed two skiffs on the horizon and, assuming they knew what they were doing, continued in their direction. As I approached, two anglers in the closest skiff started waving their arms. Then I heard yelling. The lead skiff idled toward me, and the man at the wheel—a guide, I assumed—brought his boat parallel to mine.

"Look," he'd said, trying to maintain composure, "You just drove right over the spot where tarpon come through. As long as your boat is here, they'll spook before they get to us. Just idle back behind that second boat and stake up. We take turns.

That's the way it works here." The other man, seated with his fly rod resting on his knees, glared at me.

Rich laughs. "You were *that guy,*" he says. "That asshole I'd have yelled at."

I tell Rich how, in that moment of embarrassment, I'd decided to avoid the backcountry. Ignorant to local etiquette— each tarpon spot having its own distinct protocol—I'd pissed off two guide boats and disturbed the fishing for their paying customers. When I idled in the direction from which I'd arrived, my prop wash churned up mud and turtle grass. I heard more yelling, louder this time, but didn't turn to face it. On the run home, I crossed a bank so shallow, I had to lift the motor and use the push pole—not as easy as it looks—to find deeper water. I decided then that hiring a tarpon fly-fishing guide would be worth the investment.

Rich carries an air of confidence uncommon in most 20-somethings; it borders on arrogance. His parents own a canal-side home in Islamorada, where he spent his summers as a kid. Their neighbor was the legendary tarpon angler Stu Apte. Rich learned the finer points of fly fishing for tarpon from his father and from Stu, the angler's equivalent of learning the cello from Yo-Yo Ma.

For the past several years, Rich has stayed at his family's Islamorada home from January through early June, prime tarpon season. In June, sensing the end of the migration, Rich returns to New Hampshire to help with the family business. "We deal with diamonds," he tells me.

Despite our dissimilar upbringings and my sense that our personalities could not be much different, I feel, when I'm on the casting platform, that Rich and I are teammates. He's encouraging and, unlike other Keys' guides, does not yell at or berate his anglers. He works hard to cover water and find fish. Plus, Rich has something I want—valuable knowledge of the backcountry landscape, tides, forage, and tendencies of the tarpon that live there. He doesn't care whether the fish we find are year-round residents or part of the great migration that sweeps north each spring. A tarpon is a tarpon. What matters is the stealthy approach, the accuracy of the cast, and selling the fly to a fish that might be twice our age.

Rich runs the skiff past a snowy egret standing in a few inches of water. We slow to an idle where a narrow channel splits two small grass flats. The spot looks no different than the dozens we've passed. The channel is aquamarine and streaked with silt flushing on the tide. Rich kills the motor, then climbs the poling platform.

"I don't take many people here," he says.

I can't tell if he means it or if this is just guide-speak to make me feel important. He continues: "That channel is twenty feet deep. Kind of comes out of nowhere, doesn't it? I found this spot by accident while I was permit fishing. Lots of sharks in that channel—so don't fall in. There's usually a few tarpon here."

He poles for about thirty seconds, then: "Okay Ryan, fish just rolled, sixty feet, dead ahead. I'll turn us. Make the cast when you're ready."

The sun's glare is so intense I can't see much of anything. Even behind polarized lenses, my eyes water, but I make the cast.

"OK, now strip it slowwwww," Rich says. "Good. Just like that."

I slide the fly once more and my line comes tight. I strip-set and bury the rod butt into my right hip. The loose line resting on my feet jumps and I clear it of all obstructions. The tarpon somersaults, crashes, runs—my fingers burn with the friction of fleeing fly line. I'm already into the backing. A football field away, the tarpon jumps again.

Rich hollers from the deck, "That's how we do it!" He turns the bow to face the channel, then shoves the push pole into the bottom. It feels like the scene from a movie I'm watching. "Now you have to *catch* it!" he says.

The tarpon is medium-size, maybe sixty pounds, a perfect fly-rod fish. Still, I'm conditioned to anticipate the worst: I imagine the leader will break; I imagine suffering the familiar disappointment of slack line. Rich, staying far calmer than I

Rich reviving a tarpon in Florida Bay.

am, gives instructions. I gain all of my backing and, once the fly line is back on my reel, apply maximum pressure. My line slices through the channel as the tarpon maneuvers against my pulling.

"Don't be afraid to really haul on that fish," Rich says. "Pull back against the direction it wants to go in."

The tarpon appears near the surface, forty feet away, its back blue-green iridescence. Then it tips on its side, angling away from me, its tail-kicks labored. With my fly rod pointed into the water, I pull against the fish's path, the leader paralleling the tarpon's lateral line. Startled by the line's contact, the tarpon surges and jumps one last time. I point the rod tip to the jump, imparting slack to save my leader. When the tarpon lands, I pull back even harder, turning the fish over on itself. Rich kneels at the gunwale. A few moments later, he has the leader in his gloved hand, and, after a brief struggle, the tarpon is secure. Rich grips my first tarpon on a fly by its lower jaw.

He removes the fly and starts reviving the fish. I take a few photographs with my cell phone. The tarpon's enormous side scales are silver prisms to the sunlight. He works to get water flowing over its gills, so it can swim away strongly and avoid nearby sharks. The tarpon regains strength, contorting its body and kicking its tail. Rich releases his grip. The fish rights itself and swims out of sight.

Fighting off tears of joy, I pat Rich on the back. He snips the leader and hands me the mangled fly, a meaningful souvenir. I imagine back home I'll keep the fly somewhere safe, somewhere visible. "Congratulations, man," he says, smiling. "Now let's go catch a big one."

As we run to the next spot, closer toward the dock in Islamorada, it begins to set in that I've finally accomplished my goal. The accomplishment—still surreal, in its newness—feels more like a rite of passage, like the opening of a lifelong passion, than it does a relief. Landing one on a fly confirmed that I was capable, with the help of a guide of Rich's pedigree, spotting and calling out fish as they approached, doing the hard work of positioning the boat for the best cast, keeping me in the game and keeping my confidence high; that made the difference.

Rich slows the skiff off plane, then begins to pole again. Up on the casting platform I think of all the people I'll call once I'm off the water, to tell about this day.

My very next cast, a hundred-pound tarpon inhales a fresh version of the same fly, leaps four times in succession, before my leader slips. Rich is apologetic, says the nail knot shouldn't slip like that, but I'm not upset. Unlike the blind-cast that resulted in my first tarpon on a fly, this fish was highly visible with the sun behind us. Before my cast, Rich spotted the fish, asked me if I saw "the floating battleship at two o'clock." The tarpon ate my fly with its head out of the water, like a salmon sipping a dry fly from the surface of a Maine pond.

On our ride back to the dock, Rich slows the skiff near one of the major channels close to town. In the distance, traffic streams over the bridges toward Key West, a reminder that we're making our way back toward civilization. I'm sun-dazed and thirsty, but I don't want this day to end.

"I want to check one last spot," Rich says. "They'll either be here or they won't."

He's not up on the platform long before: "Holy shit, Ryan. There's a pile of tarpon. Get ready!"

Up ahead, I see the dark, swirling meatball of tarpon. Rich poles closer.

"Go ahead," he instructs.

My first two casts are tentative and short.

"Just get it in there, man!" Rich says. The southeasterly wind is pushing the skiff past the school. I'll have one more shot.

I land the fly, strip once, then a silver flash amongst the school, and again my line is tight. A giant boil as the fish—and the group around it—startles. A massive tarpon propels itself into the air, head shaking so violently my fly line dances. The fish charges to deeper water. My reel screams. All I can do is hang on. Rich leaps down from his platform.

"That's a *monster!*" he shouts. Quickly he clips the push pole and fires up the engine.

The tarpon bulldogs into a deep channel and heads toward the ocean. I can't turn her. My forearms ache. Rich tells me to apply more pressure, "or that fish will pull us around until she dies." My fly rod flexes beyond recognition; I wait for it to shatter.

Rich maneuvers the skiff around crab pots and channel markers. We pass a pair of old timers soaking bait from an ancient Grady White. They look at us with confusion as their hands visor the sun. We're getting closer to the bridges that divide bay from open ocean. The tarpon surges and peels more line.

"If I was fighting that fish, I'd whoop its ass in twenty minutes," Rich says from behind the wheel. I try to ignore him. The tarpon turns left and leaves the channel. I haven't gained much line.

"Pull harder," Rich urges. "She's in shallow water now. She has nowhere to go."

Fifty-five minutes in, the leader parts, my line slackens, and the huge tarpon slinks over white sand. In exaltation, I watch her dark back until she disappears.

"What do you think she weighed?" I ask Rich, as he stows the fly rod in the gunnel.

"I dunno, one-thirty?" he says, "at least."

At the dock, I settle up with Rich. He's earned it. I give him a few homespun tarpon flies in appreciation, though I know he'll probably never use them. I tell him how important the day has been for me, how good it feels to finally land a tarpon on fly. We shake hands and talk about plans for next spring.

From my rental car I see Rich, still by the boat launch, standing with another, older guide, gesturing to him. The older guide is attentive, smiling. It occurs to me that Rich is telling him about our tarpon. It is satisfying to watch.

On my drive to dinner that evening, sitting in perpetual Keys' traffic, I cross the bridge over Indian Key Channel, aware it's the same spot Dad landed our first tarpon with Bruce on that full-moon night ten years ago. I ease off the pedal. To my left, the Atlantic Ocean and Indian Key, and a beached and abandoned sailboat, sits tilted on an oceanside flat. To my right, turquoise water rushes toward the backcountry. I imagine the unlucky crabs and shrimps and baitfish flushing back there on the tide. I imagine what awaits them.

Three skiffs are anchored near the bridge. The sun is behind the skiffs, immense and low in the sky. Tarpon baits in the water, the guides and their clients are silhouettes anxiously waiting for a bite.

THE SWEET SPOT

Past the Far East Restaurant, and Big Daddy's Buff n' Wax, we turn left at the Mexico Congregational Church and find the boat launch empty. This is normal here but surprises me on a fine spring morning: the Androscoggin River is at its most fishable level—around 4,500 cubic feet per second (cfs)—plus it's free fishing weekend in Maine, and the river's numerous, overweight smallmouth should be holding tight to the banks. We unload the canoe, neither of us complain about lack of company.

My good friend, Parker, is running on Red Bull and three hours' sleep, while I'm trying not to think of my guide-trip the following day, given the rain, wind, and 40-degree temperatures forecasted. Today is a different story: upper-60s, few fair-weather cumulus, new leaves on shoreline maples and birches. I've talked this section up to Parker for years, but this is our first chance to fish it together. We'll float seven miles from Mexico down to Dixfield, past the Catalyst Paper mill, behind Walmart, alongside the Maine Central Railroad, over some of the best smallmouth water in the state.

Across the river, which is wide and swift-moving here at the put-in, the mill that once killed off all aquatic river life emits a steady hum. Morning sun lights the largest of four smokestacks—the one closest to the river—its business end rust-tinged like the water rushing by. The air smells faintly of sulfur. As we gear up, I'm reminded of stories of mill fumes peeling paint off nearby houses. That was before my lifetime, but recent enough that plenty of locals still remember. Directly below the smokestack, deep water runs along a sandy bank.

Parker, sporting his lucky red Tackle Shop hat, polarized sunglasses, sunshirt emblazoned with a tarpon print, takes the bow, gripping his four-weight and a chartreuse ostrich herl fly with hunter-orange barbell eyes. He is the ideal candidate for the front seat, given that I outweigh him by about seventy-five pounds, and given that he stands a foot shorter than me. I'm used to fishing this way: caster in front and boat handler in back. It's how Dad and I fished when I was younger, how we still fish, chasing salmon on Pierce Pond and trout on the Kennebec. We pass riffles holding stocked rainbows and head toward the mill side of the river, paddling a little too fast, driven by our shared enthusiasm.

I steer the canoe close enough to the sandy bank that Parker's underpowered rod can reach, but not so close we spook fish off their holds. Parker's first casts are awkward, his loops open up, and his fly smacks the river.

"Little rusty," he says.

"Slow everything down," I say. "Take your time."

It's only his third season fly-casting, and he's still working out the kinks. One of his bad habits is his tendency to rush the rod tip forward, as if he's launching a swimbait on a spinning setup, rather than stopping the tip and letting his rod do the work. He's good about taking suggestions, and I offer a few more without wanting to overwhelm or irritate him. His fly plops like a fallen acorn.

"This spot looks so fishy," Parker says, stripping the fly with erratic bumps, watching the end of his floating line. He's adept at working bucktails and soft plastics for stripers, so he's not afraid to fish slowly.

We're both standing in the canoe, which takes some getting used to. Parker balances, his shoulders hunched like a linebacker, though, if he played football, which I would advise him against, he'd be the placekicker. Like me, he's fair skinned and freckled, with dark hair and a beard, though he's not losing his hair like I am. Parker could pass for my younger brother, which is fitting since he might be the only person I know who loves fishing more than I do.

Parker strip-sets, pauses, thinks he's stuck bottom. Then bottom swims upstream, and a smallmouth pushing three pounds leaps with the fly fixed to the corner of its mouth. Parker's four-weight arches into the river. The bass doesn't take much line but pulls toward deeper water. The current swings the bow downstream. Parker works the fish as best he can. When it tires, which takes a while in the cool water, he lifts it to the surface and guides it to the net.

"What a fish," he says, supporting the bass by its distended belly, likely loaded with crayfish, and eggs.

"Bigger than most of those rat stripers you like to catch," I say. He laughs.

Quickly we take a few photos, then Parker revives the bass, and it dives deep. He rinses his hands in the river, then stands back up, ready for another cast.

"Thank you," he says, and I can tell he means it.

I met Parker at The Tackle Shop, back when it was still on India Street, in downtown Portland. He helped me find fly-tying materials that first day, for tarpon flies probably, and we talked fishing for a while, then exchanged numbers. What I remember about him from early in our friendship was his warmth—always optimistic, up for anything, eager to share information, no show-off-y bullshit or bragging or Instagram hero photos. He was still learning the basics of fly-casting, and he'd spent most of his early sessions spin-fishing for stripers in the southern Maine surf near his hometown of South Portland. I could tell he was a little green and eager to learn.

Like me, Parker had one older sister, but unlike me, his father didn't fish much. The Tackle Shop owner, Dana, had taken Parker under his wing and given him a summer job at the shop. I worked there for a while too, just a day or two a week for a summer. We stayed in touch, exchanged fish pictures, and eventually made plans to fish together.

The first time we did, I took Parker to one of the toughest dry-fly fisheries in Maine (classified, sorry). I wanted him to witness the place, which was my favorite to fish in all of Maine, aside from Pierce Pond. When he saw the size of the trout's dorsal fins, as the fish rose all around our canoe, he lost his cool. He rushed his casts, which fell short of target, over and over again. His back casts slapped the river and spooked the trout. His leaders knotted from his tailing loop. He just couldn't get it done. It was hard to watch the repeated failures and spooked fish, but I knew how tough the river could be. The bar had been set, and rather than shy away from it or hang his head, Parker acknowledged defeat.

"Well, that was an ass-kicking," he said, at the end of that first evening. "But I'm glad I saw it. That was incredible. I can't wait to come back, after some practice."

Over the next few years, Parker worked on his casting, alone and with me, making technical improvements that added distance and accuracy. Soon he could land a fly accurately at fifty feet, with only the occasional backslap or tangled leader. It was satisfying to watch his progress. It had taken me years to

Parker working his fly back toward the canoe.

get comfortable throwing a fly line and I knew only time and repetition would get him there.

We returned to that same river many times. It took him a few more trips, but the first time he landed a trout there, which was close to four pounds, we went to a bar in Solon. With black bear and moose mounts watching from the walls, I bought Parker a celebratory whiskey.

When we get back up there, which is not often these days, with Parker married and working fifty-hour weeks, and me teaching and writing and dating, he lands a good trout nearly every time. I wonder if I feel the same or similar satisfaction as Dad did, watching me fail and then return, over and over, until success became a kind of expectation for us both.

A half-mile downstream we float beneath a rusted footbridge, then the Veteran's Street Bridge. We pass more smokestacks with white steam clouds hanging in the still air. Parker lands a few smaller bass as we reach the end of the mill complex. A squeaking conveyor belt resembling a skyward roller coaster deposits bald logs in a massive pile.

This section of the Androscoggin lacks the attributes anglers expect from Maine rivers: banks lined with leaning hardwoods and the occasional split-log camp, not to mention native salmonids. It's a delicate conversation with inquiring clients of mine: we could fish the classic water, I tell them, the Magalloway, or Kennebago, where we might encounter a big brookie or salmon, and where we'll certainly find anglers fishing the same, day-long circuit. (I pause, then, for effect.) *Or* we could leave the waders at home and fish the Andro from my canoe, put in across from the mill and float over more sunken tires than you've ever seen, past the shopping cart behind the big island that usually has a bass over it, through a forest of submerged vinyl folding chairs. We'll lose count of odd debris sightings, and of caught fish. Big, fat, mean bass. Knot-testers. It might stink a little, too—the air in the upper valley, I mean, not the fishing. There's an occasional drift boat on weekends, the odd kayaker, or worm-dunker wading in from Route 4, but usually we fish this water alone.

A half-mile beyond the mill-complex, the river starts to change. It's subtle at first, a narrowing where the current picks up and carries us away from town, as if the Androscoggin herself wants us rushed toward wilder parts. Soon we're casting at tangled roots along freshly eroded banks, fallen trees still hanging onto green leaves. Parker hooks a big fish on the drop and somehow yards it out of underwater branches. The bass jumps and pukes crayfish parts in various stages of digestion. It dives under the canoe and Parker nearly dumps us following the fish with his rod tip. The bass takes up most of the net.

We maneuver the canoe out of a tree that pinned us in the mayhem, and then Parker spots a bald eagle perched in a shoreline tree. The massive bird appears black against green foliage, with an impossibly yellow hooked beak. It watches us with an air of nonchalance. I wonder how many fish have met their fate under that beak. From across the river, the high-pitched piping of another eagle. Already, the mill feels far behind.

The river bends sharply eastward, and we're surrounded by green rolling hills. We pass rocky islands, navigate minor rapids, kick up a raft of wood ducks, and pass a great blue heron standing rigid as a totem pole. Parker feeds a few more bass, medium-sized. He switches from streamer to popper to streamer again. It doesn't matter today; they'll eat anything. A train car chugs by, headed for the mill, and the conductor leans out and waves.

"Let me play guide for a bit," Parker says later, and, despite my reluctance to give up the stern, I take the opportunity.

I love smallmouth for their forgiveness. I botch a few hook sets—setting too early—but then get back into form. I prospect steep banks, eddies behind rocks, riffles at the edges of drop offs, and the bass reward me. Parker nets them. Satiated, I'm soon back at the stern, my guide instincts taking over, preferring to watch a good friend fish water I've grown familiar with, and attached to.

At Lunch Island, walking the canoe over a shallow gravel bar, I nearly squish a crayfish as it scuds between stones. We eat turkey sandwiches and look out over the river in silence. No boats pass. I think of how easy it would be to dub this river a success story, how that label would be both truthful and misleading. How, in the sixties, chemicals from the logging industry settled over this riverbed, killed first the vegetation, then the insects, then the dace, trout, salmon, eagles. How the Androscoggin was ranked among the most-polluted rivers in the country. How the river came back, with help from the Clean Water Act and a reseeding of bass. How they got fat on crayfish. But the trout still don't summer well because oxygen depletion remains a problem. On some days, yellow foam still eddies out on the sides of the Androscoggin.

Stepping out of the canoe in the wrong place on this stretch has buried me up to my knees in goop. It smells sulfuric, and tickling bubbles boil up. Beneath that layer—if one were inclined to dig—lies a void, a lifeless stratum. Below that, maybe an ancient fishing hook, or an arrowhead. Above the goop, now, underwater grasses and mossy rocks, with stonefly cases clinging, and crayfish defending themselves with claws upraised, bass tipped down and feeding. This is what I'm imagining as we finish lunch, push off in the canoe, and continue downstream.

Parker probing the bank for bass while I steady the canoe.

Four locals lob bass plugs from the bank where the Webb River tumbles in. We skip the pool and paddle hard cross-current. Beyond an old concrete slab of unknown origin, a spent red oxygen tank, and a rusty oil drum, a wide-mouthed stream meets the river.

"They'll lay right on that sandbar, at the mouth," I say, back-paddling to slow the canoe. Parker lays out a perfect cast.

"You mean, right *there?*" he says, in a rare flash of cockiness, Parker setting the hook on a big fish that pulls line and thrashes its head. He has his hands full with the four-weight.

"That's excellent guiding right there," I say.

"I'll try not to fuck it up."

The bass finally comes to net, sporting an old hook injury that hasn't slowed its eating habits. It's the heaviest fish of the day.

We paddle hard through dead water to the last pool, a boulder field with a rock as big as a cabin. We're too tired for small talk and, after Parker lands another bass, we silently call it a day and paddle for the take-out. We know, without saying anything, that we've hit it right, the season's sweet spot.

We round the last bend, the landing now in sight. I remind myself to call my client later and arrange a meeting time for the morning. For some reason, I find it more satisfying to friend-guide, compared to the pressures and paranoias of guiding for cash. It's not a great business model, but I love showing good friends new water. For a few moments, near the very end of the run, we stop paddling and let the current carry us.

"You know, in the ten years I've guided here, I've never fished beyond this take-out."

Parker turns in his seat, looks beyond me, back up the river valley. He says, "Yeah, but why would you even want to?"

It occurs to me, as the canoe slides into shoreline grasses at the take-out, that something less obvious than great fishing draws me back here. Perhaps the pull is in part the valley's complex history, its resiliency in the face of industrial pollution, the river's constant effort to flush its messy past out to sea. More likely, I'm drawn to the Androscoggin's imperfections: strange artifacts along its banks, juxtaposition of mill-complex and beautiful boulder pools, and still, the bass existing—thriving, even—here at the murky confluence of industry and wildness.

And I'm happy to have shared the river with Parker, especially this stretch. I know he'll keep it to himself. It is a kind of unspoken trust we've built over the years, sharing our spots without worry, knowing the other will keep it close. After we drag the canoe to my truck, Parker thanks me for paddling, shakes my hand, and gives me a hug. We remind each other to exchange fish pictures from the day, and he wishes me luck guiding. Then we get in our respective trucks and leave the take-out.

The next time we fish here together—next summer, maybe—the water will have dropped, the riverbed revealing more of itself, more of the valley's complicated history. The resilient bass will be off the banks, then down deep in the oxygenated water while it lasts, harder to find and fool. But I suspect Parker will have added a few more feet to his cast, that we'll be ready for the challenge. Maybe I'll take a few more shots up front, but I doubt it.

ALLAGASHED: HOW TO CATCH A MAINE MUSKIE

When you run out of highway, in Sherman, take Route 11 North. There's Mt. Katahdin to the west, summit capped by a thin blade of cloud like the edge of a giant gill plate. In Patten, avoid Amish wagons—be thankful for your kind of horsepower. Pass the Masardis lumber mill, the Portage country store that looks transported from the sixties. Do we have enough gas to get there? Dad wants to know. More houses now, an elementary school, and Fort Kent, sign for "America's First Mile," the start of Route 1. Think of its southern terminus, Key West, and wish for a moment you'd driven that direction instead—permit, bonefish, tarpon! Refuel. Pass the border crossing to Canada, a nondescript bridge, patrol cars, no lines. Notice the wide, flat, St. John River beneath, so bony you could flee your country with dry knees.

Then, 341 miles north of Portland, arrive at Tylor Kelly Camps, in the town of Allagash, at the confluence of the Allagash and St. John Rivers. Your cabin from the outside is no frills. It is unlocked. Go on in, unload your gear, fill the fridge. Couches,

TV, open kitchen, two bedrooms, each with bunkbeds. Six whitetail mounts watch from the walls. Books on brook trout and bear hunting. Flip through guestbook: "Saw a few muskie, very exciting!" and "Shot nice boar, caught muskie same week, great trip." String up the eight-weight and the ten, intermediate sink and float, select flies, place rods on rack, all before unpacking your suitcase—priorities! "Seems like mostly hunters stay here," you say.

"We might cast to fish that have never seen a fly," Dad counters.

Feel good about your chances.

Loud knock at the door. In comes Wade: owner, guide, moose and bear expert, muskie catcher. He welcomes you, knows you're self-guiding, but is happy to share his insights. Has guided over thirty years here, about the time muskie have been in these waters, invaders from Canada. Still figuring them out, Wade says. Yes, they're in the Little Black, yes, in the Allagash, up to The Falls, yes, the St. John, too. They tend to eat flies better than lures, he says.

Try to remain calm. Instead, fantasize about becoming a renowned Maine muskie guide. Discoverer of untapped fishery—the fish of fifty casts! Listen to options Wade offers and decide to float the Little Black River the next morning, remote, rarely fished. Hard access, so there's a transportation fee, not cheap. Wade will haul canoe and gear, drive you both in, drop you off so you can float downstream to confluence with the St. John. And oh yes, did he mention his client caught a mid-forty-incher on fly in the Little Black last week? That no one has fished it since? Shake Wade's hand. Exchange excited, you've-got-to-be-kidding-me look with Dad. Go to bed early.

Try hard to sleep, but instead picture golden torpedoes stalking your fly and vicious, toothy bites.

Wade is thirty minutes early, but you are both up and ready. It's an hour's drive from where you leave your truck at the take-out. From there, paved road turns to dirt, thoroughfare to logging road, past gates operated by timber companies. A walkie-talkie dangles from Wade's dash, radio on so he can hear chatter from oncoming pulp trucks, to be avoided. He makes enough turns that you could never retrace the route. As he drives, Wade tells stories of catching muskie in riffles he fished as a kid for salmon. He's trying to make a living up here, at the crown of Maine, adapting to a changing environment, to changes beyond his control. Would he prefer the muskie not be here? Of course. Will he fight to promote the muskie fishery, *and* preserve what's left of brook trout waters? You bet. Most of his clients are bear or moose hunters, but more and more, folks are coming for muskie. A Canadian muskie guide, for example, takes a week's vacation here in late summer, and last year he had a twenty-fish day, which would be a hell of a year of muskie fishing.

What Wade's driving on now is more of a game trail than a passable road. Stunted pines encroach the truck, which bounces and rocks through dried brooks and a crater that could swallow a sedan. Move to the edge of your seat and grab the roof handle. Start to understand and validate the transport fee—Wade is earning every penny, branches gouging his truck's side panels. You see the mist before you see the river. It rises and hangs in the morning air like the breath of some hidden forest monster. Wade pulls onto a rocky bar beside the river, which is slow-moving, slightly tannic, lined by tall, spiky firs. Just wide enough for a back-cast. It occurs to you that this is—or was—essentially a trout stream, and Wade confirms: farther upstream you can still find a few fat brookies, but this section has been commandeered by muskellunge. Unload the canoe and fill it with gear and fly

rods. Take a cast through that run, Wade says, pointing. He's
seen big ones taken from it. A couple false casts, and your fly is
dancing through the current. All three of you watch, transfixed—
it couldn't happen on the first cast, could it? It doesn't. Wade
approves of your set-up.

"You'll get one today," he says.

Wade gets back in his truck, shifts in gear, then disappears,
his Ford swallowed by the Maine woods, leaving you and Dad
alone at the river's edge.

Paddle upstream a while, through dead water framed by
alders and deadfalls, Dad up front. From the middle of the river,
cover both banks. How quickly you fall into rhythm: cast, strip,
lift, repeat. This is not dredging for brook trout or smallmouth—
there's palpable tension, knowing each cast could lure something
monstrous. Dad chucks his fly near a beaver dam, works it back
to the bow with erratic strips. As he's lifting his rod to recast, a
muskie slashes his fly. Dad's looking elsewhere when it happens,
so you shout, but it's too late. He sees the boil settling boatside.

"Sleepin' on the job!" he says.

The river reminds you that you're muskie fishing. An hour
passes, no more follows. You guide the canoe through fishy
riffles, around sharp rocks that would put a dent in your day.

Dad has to piss, so you beach the canoe on a sand spit,
and he steps out and stretches. When you exit the canoe, your
wading boot lands atop an old bear track, direct hit. The tracks
weather-worn but you can make out the pads and claws, the
depth of imprint an indication of the bear's weight. You sense
the wildness of the place and wonder for a second if anything is
watching you.

Grab a snack from the cooler, rehydrate. Dad wants the back seat so you can take some casts. Two moose flies the size of hummingbirds orbit your head as if daring the other to land. Dad pulls a leech from his sandal and then you push off, navigate rocks in a small rapid, and you're fishing again.

From the stern Dad drags his fly through a deep, swift-moving pool and for some reason you're looking back at his fly as it crosses a shallow hump. He's essentially trolling, and you can't blame him; your shoulder is tired from all the casting. As you watch his fly wiggle, a muskie rolls but misses it. Dad yanks the fly.

"Shit!" he says.

Pull off in an eddy and reposition the canoe. Dad wants you to take the shot—yes, he's sure—he's missed enough of them today. You'd rushed through the pool so quickly it's hard to know where the fish came from. "Sure wanted that fly," Dad says. You make your best guess and throw, get tight to the fly, and work it back with two hands. Your fly swims like a wounded chartreuse eel.

The strike is an upward sweep. You watch the muskie rise from the sand and eat. When you strike back, the muskie darts upstream. Let it run. Pray your fifty-pound fluorocarbon leader clears its upper-jaw razors. Gain back line. Near the canoe the muskie rolls, wrapping itself in line. Dad grabs the net but misses his first swipe. The muskie surges again, then tires. When it meets the net, it rolls, spins, tangles itself. Its length and girth seem disproportionate to the narrow river in which it has grown.

Beach the canoe and fumble for the camera bag, hands shaking. Exchange fist bump with Dad. How big is it? As usual, Dad guesses high and you guess realistically, or so you think. You're both wrong. It's not forty inches, but close, one trout-snack away.

Remove the fly from its corner jaw with your bare hand—
carefully, carefully. Grip the fat nub near its tail with one hand
and slide the fingers of your other below its gills. Turn toward
the sun and lift. Photos won't do it justice. Its back is a green-
brown camouflage, its flank mottled bronze. When you release
it, the muskie slides over sandy bottom, blends in perfectly and
disappears. You wonder how many fish you've paddled over,
how many followed unbeknownst or had already eaten and thus
granted your fly a free pass.

Some Mainers would throw that muskie up on the bank
to rot. You've heard Mainers talk about muskellunge—of their
introduction, of management options, of the threat they pose to
the Allagash Waterway and the native brook trout and salmon.
They're as divisive as the two-party system. You rinse your hands
in the river and get back in the canoe. Can you fish for and enjoy
muskellunge and native brook trout, without being a hypocrite,
you wonder? Can you help curb the spread of invasives but
take advantage of their presence? And when does a fish become
native? Is forty years' residency enough? Fifty?

You fish a few more pools, deep and swirling. Dad has a
follow but the big muskie never closes the gap, slinks to the
bottom without striking. By now the sun is high and hot. You
come around a bend and along the shore there's a deer—but
no—wrong color. It occurs to you that it's a moose but appears
too small—a moose in miniature. And it is: a calf the color of
caramel, maybe fifty pounds, wading the shoreline. Thirty yards
up the bank, its mother sticks her colossal head through an
opening in the bush and bellows a warning, aimed at you or her
offspring, it's unclear.

Stop paddling and let the current carry you closer. The
cow turns and lumbers off, branches snap and shatter under the
weight of her retreat. Her calf stands in the river. It is not much

bigger than your Labrador, the one you put down a week ago, who'd made it to the doorstep of fifteen. The calf spots you but doesn't know what to make of your approach. It stumbles downstream, mewing and whimpering. You pass at thirty feet, so close you can see its eyes, blueish-white at the center, like a blind soothsayer's. There's something haunting about the calf's eyes, about its helplessness and vulnerability, and you keep thinking of it long after you've rounded the next bend.

"That was something," Dad says, and for a while fishing seems secondary.

When you reach the truck, you are sun-weary yet satisfied. You and Dad haul the canoe up the bank and soon you're driving back to the cabin. It feels like success, landing a nice muskie on a fly and moving a few others under the bright Maine sun, satisfaction compounded by a moose sighting and bear tracks, by being alone with your father on new water in the middle of nowhere. While Dad naps, you marvel at the ability of wilderness to strip away the superfluous, and how a quest to find a certain fish often morphs into a different story altogether.

The next day, fish the Allagash River. Dad tells you how he paddled the ninety-plus-mile waterway with his father before you were born, when his father was the same age he is now. If there were muskie then, he hadn't known. They caught brook trout in the evenings to cook over an open fire. You think of how rivers and fish and the lives of anglers intersect, of how water preserves fragments of memory. Your grandfather is twenty years gone but then what are two decades to an ancient river?

A few ragged-looking canoe paddlers pass, gawking as you sling your eight-inch fly cross-current. You catch a small muskie on the swing in a riffle—salmon water— then another, medium-sized, in a slow-moving, rocky pool. A canoer lunching on shore

watches through binoculars as you release the second fish back
into the river. Dad casts and casts, but nothing doing.

On the drive back to the cabin, stop to walk a road-side pool
Wade recommended. Dad wanders downstream with his rod
as you cast methodically. Cover water, watch for follows. What
an appropriate name, you think, the *muskellunge*: its first two
syllables lulling you to sleep like the hot summer sun and then
the final *-lunge,* surging forward as if to inhale a fly.

Dad shouts from downstream. You watch him figure-eight at
his feet, his rod a sword carving the river. A muskie wakes his fly
in a foot of water. "Got him!" he yells, but when he lifts his rod
there's no bend.

Scramble over stones to hear his story: "Damn thing just
came out of nowhere! I didn't see it until it was right behind
my fly and it kept following and then it just sat there watching
and I didn't know what the hell to do but keep my fly moving I
thought it ate but it only nipped the fly's tail it was bigger than
the one you got yesterday but the damn hook didn't stick!"

Listen attentively as he retells the story on the short ride back
to the cabin. "I keep seeing that fish in my mind," he says later,
over dinner, calm but sounding haunted, as if he's been visited
by a ghost.

The next morning, rise early and pack the truck. Wade stops
by to drop off the bill and see how you'd done on the Allagash;
he's happy you've caught a few. Dad says he'd like to come back
next year, maybe go farther up the Little Black, camp along it,
make it an overnight trip. Wade thinks it's a good idea, says he'd
be happy to drive you in and drop you off.

Finish packing. Try to ignore the nagging, fear-based
question that arises in your mind at the end of every trip
together: was this one our last?

Before you leave the cabin, Dad says, "Don't forget to sign the guestbook."

So you write your names and: "Three muskies on fly in two full days of fishing and moved a handful more. Saw bear tracks, a moose calf and mother, and no other anglers. We'll be back."

A DAY ON THE ICE

When Danny called me around Christmas from his administrative desk at an Ivy League school, he sounded polite, even a bit shy, explaining he found my number on the Maine Guide Registry. He and his group of friends—late twenty-somethings, professionals—were planning a trip to Maine in early March. They wanted to try something new together, and ice fishing seemed like a novel experience.

It would be seven of them. All except Danny lived and worked in Manhattan, and many had graduated from Ivy League schools. A few had fished before, he thought, but none had ever ice-fished. The group had met as teenagers, attending a Jewish summer camp in central Maine, on the shore of East Pond, part of which extended into my hometown, Smithfield, where I first learned to fish. I wondered if we'd all been on the water together, years before, without even knowing it.

I told Danny that, as their guide, it was my job to supply breakfast, lunch, drinks, along with all needed fishing gear, portable shelter, propane heater, and snowmobiles for transportation.

"What should we wear? I'm assuming it'll be pretty cold," he said.

"Layers," I said. "Pack boots, if possible, with a good pair of woolen socks. It's always better to overdress. It could be forty degrees, or it could be zero."

I gave him our fishing options: we could fish a lake with plenty of action, but the fish would be small. In that scenario, we would keep some pan fish—perch or black crappie—to fry up for lunch. Or we could target much larger, invasive northern pike. In the second scenario, I explained, there was more risk involved. It was more like trophy hunting, so success was not guaranteed. We would set our baits and hope for the best, but it might not happen. On a good day, we might only catch a pike or two, but they would be bigger than any fish he and his friends had likely ever seen.

"Let me ask the guys," Danny said. "But I'm guessing they'll want to try for pike."

He called back a few days later: the consensus was in. We confirmed for a Saturday in early March, to go northern pike fishing in Belgrade.

Northern pike—illegally introduced to Maine waters in the late seventies—are apex predators capable of ingesting prey up to half their body weight. When big females push twenty or twenty-five pounds, it's understandable why they pass up a live shiner for something more substantial, such as the twenty-inch brown trout in the belly of a twenty-two pounder I once landed, or a diving duck—an adult merganser, in another, caught by the friend of a friend.

The experience of guiding for pike is both frustrating and exhilarating. Entire winter days have passed, with prevailing northwesterlies shifting snow about the ice, covering holes I've drilled, as if to taunt my efforts. The pike bite unpredictably, and less so on windy bright days, though often just often enough to keep one's interest. "It only takes one," I repeat, not really believing anymore, as I wait with anxious, shivering clients.

A day of guiding on the ice rarely goes as planned. There are too many variables beyond one's control—weather patterns, atmospheric pressure, angling pressure—for predictability. When I book an ice fishing trip, I often experience dueling thrill and palpable anxiety. Will the clients leave exhilarated, satisfied, disappointed? Will they return to fish with me again?

I've gone fishless on numerous pike trips, some with negative wind-chill, snow-buried tip-ups, and disheartened clients. I run out of stories to tell, out of general entertainment, out of food to cook; then it's just me, and one or two strangers, and the wind ripping by. *Thank you for your suffering,* I think, *that will be four-hundred dollars.*

The evening before the trip with Danny's crew, I drive my snowmobile onto Messalonskee Lake's shallow, weedy, horseshoe-shaped south bay. A north-south lake nine miles long, Messalonskee is barren, save a smattering of ice shacks.

The freeze/thaw pattern of March has reduced winter's heavy snowfall to small, wind-packed dunes. The bay resembles a frozen, whitewashed desert, or a deleted scene from *Fargo.* I cross fresh snowmobile tracks, pass augured holes skimmed with ice. Beside the holes, discarded shiners that eagles or coyotes will scavenge by morning.

Prepping for the next day, I drill twenty-five holes, roughly fifty feet apart. My forearms ache after the last few, given the shock absorption from the rattling auger, and because there is over two feet of ice to drill through. I clear slush with a skimmer and mark each hole with cedar boughs to make them easy to find in the morning. Now that the holes are dug and marked, I can slip in early, quietly, and chip away the night's thin skin of ice.

Sleep that night is fitful. When I wake far too early, my thoughts tumble with planning details: ice traps, bait, auger, snowmobiles, shelter, stove, propane tanks, fry pan, food. My alarm blares at four a.m., but I am already wide awake.

Messalonskee Lake is windless, the eastern horizon a gold and purple band above shoreline pines. I make a few snowmobile runs back and forth from the landing, dropping two piles of equipment between the holes I'd dug. I am relieved to be first on the lake.

Danny and company arrive at the landing a half hour late in a caravan of SUVs, their arrival obvious even from a half-mile away. On the short ride in from the lake, I feel the familiar build of anticipation and anxiety I always feel in the moments before meeting new clients.

When I reach the landing, seven men stand clustered by my truck. Three wear blue jeans—to call them skinny jeans would be an exaggeration, but still in the ballpark. A few don thin hiking boots. Most of the crew appear vastly under-dressed for the 15-degree morning. The only other person at the landing is a lone fisherman in off-white coveralls offloading his four-wheeler from his truck. With his plaid Mad Bomber hat pulled down over his ears, he rubber-necks at the sight of us.

I approach and introduce myself, Danny coming forward first—Danny, the trip-planner—even more shy in person than on the phone. He introduces the rest of the gang: I catch the names Dan, Ben, Aaron, Anthony, missing the rest. I tell them I'd try to learn their names by the end of the day, but no guarantees. In the small sea of white Jewish New Yorkers, Anthony—a Black MIT grad—stands out. It occurs to me, a thought that I keep to myself, that we are the most diverse group of ice fishermen on any Maine lake.

Meanwhile, the Mainer in the plaid Bomber hat passes on his four-wheeler, gives me a head nod, and it's as if he knows my predicament, and I can almost hear him say, *Ayuh, good luck with that*—as he ventures onto the lake, dragging his dogsled of tip-ups.

The New Yorkers follow me to my snowmobiles like a raft of ducklings. Chattering amongst themselves, they carry backpacks, cameras with oversize lenses, plastic bags full of—who knows. They hold cell phones up to the sunrise. I give Aaron a quick lesson on the throttle and brake of the rear sled, since he'll follow my lead on the second snowmobile I'd kept by the road.

As the New Yorkers crowd onto both sleds, I mine for enthusiasm. I wish Parker was here to offset my angst and to help manage the newbies. They seem happy enough, though I already feel responsible for the quality of their experience, feel the full weight of it now that they've arrived.

The sun has risen above the pines but the air is still night-chilled. I am setting our third tip-up, attaching the flag by its O-ring tip to the tripper that will release with the pull of a pike, when the first tip-up I've set springs.

Underneath the ice, a northern pike, I hope, has taken the bait, pulled line, and triggered the forest-green flag to unfurl. The rectangular felt flag pointing skyward gives me a jolt of optimism. An early pike would take the pressure off and capture the crew's attention.

I yell "Flag!" to the guys, who stand huddled like penguins near my canvas pop-up shelter, fifty yards away. They turn collectively and stare. I can't blame them for their lack of understanding—they don't know better. Again I yell it, as if it is the only word in my vocabulary: *Flag!* This is the golden call of ice fishing, the one word that, when announced, brings Maine ice anglers running; men who run at no other time of year, unless chased, dropping jig-poles, Pabst cans, cribbage cards, stumbling at full speed to the sprung flag, a beacon of hope and possibility, a sudden warmth amidst the coldness of winter. I wave them on.

Earlier, I had given the group a quick hook-setting tutorial: hand-over-hand until the line comes tight and—only when you feel the weight of the fish—set the hook with a short, upward wrist snap. Keep the pressure on, no slack, but be ready to concede line when it runs. The bigger the pike, the longer the runs—long, violent dashes, line grooving the bottom of the ice.

Danny steps forward timidly, the chosen one, ready to address the tripped flag.

I lift the wooden tip-up and hand it to Anthony, volunteering to man the spool, an important task should the pike take a sudden run.

Danny bends his knees like a batter in the batter's box, readying himself above the hole. I hand him the beige line. The line comes tight, he sets the hook, and the crowd takes a collective step closer, inspecting the black portal from which no one knows what might appear.

Danny fights the pike well, with caution, lets it take line when it wants to, piling line on the ice otherwise, until a big snout appears at the bottom of the hole.

I reach my hand into the icy lake, water up to my elbow, soaking through my flannel shirt. It is not warm. My fingers find the soft underside of the jaw, slide inside, and I lift the ten-pound pike—thirty-plus inches of fish—from its ice-capped world into the bright morning air.

The crowd gasps. A few applaud, a few laugh. Danny smiles shyly and admires his catch from a safe distance.

I hold the pike up for pictures. Everyone is talking at once. Ben marvels at the colors of the pike's broad tail, the fire-orange stripes. Anthony comments on the tip-up's craftsmanship and efficiency. I point out the razor-sharp teeth protruding from the pike's lower jaw, and the multiple rows of jagged teeth on the top. I congratulate Danny.

As guide, especially tasked with managing non-anglers on an angling trip in harsh conditions, one must consider the value of providing entertainment. In the moment, it seems like a good idea to show off the pike's teeth to my clients—they have never seen anything like it, I'm sure.

So I encourage Danny to touch a single, daunting tooth on the pike's lower jaw.

"Won't it bite?" he asks.

"No way, just touch it quickly, it won't bite you," I say.

Danny steps forward, eyeing the pike's teeth, which are numerous and eerily translucent. I hold the fish horizontally, supporting the head and distended belly. Danny reaches toward the gaping mouth with his pointer finger but before he makes contact, he tips backward, like a summer camp trust fall, except there's no one there to catch him. He smacks the ice with a *thud*. Danny is out cold.

I worry I have killed my client, which will effectively end my guiding career. The thought is fleeting, but I acknowledge it: "Beloved New Yorker Dies After Maine Guide Encourages Pike Petting," the headline might read. The crew gasps, a few shout his name. I rifle through my layers to find my cell phone so I can call for help.

For about thirty seconds, Danny lies on the ice as if he's fallen asleep making snow angels. His arms are rigid and his hands curled. He is not epileptic, I am told by his friends, nor does anyone recall him having unexplained seizures. When I ask if he's diabetic, no one knows for sure, but they don't think so.

I find my phone, readying myself for the operator's questions: south end of Messalonskee Lake, late-twenties male, passed out, yes, he appears to be breathing, and I'm about to dial 911, when Danny's eyelids flutter open.

He sits up slowly, aided by his friends, then rests his elbows on his knees to reconnoiter. "What happened?" he says, sounding embarrassed. I am relieved to hear his voice.

"I think the teeth really got to you," Anthony says, not sarcastically, in the tone of a concerned friend. There is a collective sigh, and then, once we realize he's fine, that he's not dead after all, much laughter.

By noon we've landed four more pike, including a fat fifteen-pounder that gives up after one half-hearted run, a beautiful fish with vermiculate yellow-gold patterns on its gill plate. We all marvel at its size. The guys keep it for dinner back at their rental cabin. Aaron, who caught the pike, is convinced, after the five-minute battle, that his hands are frostbitten. He ambles back toward the shelter, another of the guys (whose name I never learn) walks with him, rubbing Aaron's hands with his and, once in a while, blowing on them as hard as possible.

Danny is the brunt of jokes, as one might expect, the group telling him to look away every time a pike is lifted from the lake. He is a good sport about it. It is the first time he's ever passed out, he tells me, once the morning has settled and we find our way back to the shelter. It occurs to me that because we've had so much action—ten or so tripped flags by late morning—I haven't been able to set more than seven tip-ups, out of the twenty-five I've brought along. Soon it's lunchtime.

Perhaps downwind of the moose stew bubbling over the flame of the Coleman stove, our neighbor in the plaid Bomber hat stops by. He is the coverall-wearing angler who passed us at the landing, and he introduces himself as Derrick, looking each of the New Yorkers in the eyes and shaking their hands in the brief yet sincere manner of Mainers greeting those from away.

The flaps of his hat are lifted to expose his ears. He sports a walrus mustache and fogged-up eyeglasses that look too narrow for his chubby face. Underneath his once-white coveralls, an incongruent, royal blue sweatshirt. Camouflage binoculars hang from his neck, and, now and then, he uses them to pan his own traps, set a few hundred yards away from ours.

"You boys been having some morning," Derrick says. The guys take turns recounting the highlights, Derrick listening intently, validating their excitement every few moments with an affirming, "Yehhh."

When they finish updating Derrick, he says, "Must be beginner's luck. I haven't had so much as a flag."

Anthony points Derrick to the fifteen-pounder, flopped on the ice like a baby seal. Ben has gutted the pike, which has, in death, lost intensity of color except for its still-vibrant orange tail. Derrick walks over to inspect the catch.

I dish moose stew into paper bowls, offering some to Derrick who politely declines, then I join him at the pike gut pile. Among the pike's stomach contents: a long, thin, partially digested baitfish with an iridescent sheen.

"What do you suppose that is?" I ask Derrick. "Kind of looks like a saltwater fish."

"Sure does," he says. "Almost looks like a herring."

The crew gathers back at the shelter, quiet and content with their steaming bowls of stew. One of them, the one whose name I never learn, the one who tells me, in the most deadpan monotone imaginable, that he is a stand-up comedian—walks over, holding his bowl of stew.

"Did you happen to bring any salt?" he asks.

"I did not."

He turns and walks back to his friends.

When he's out of earshot, Derrick leans in close.

"All of them queer or is it just that one of 'em?"

"I think they're just from the city," I say.

Derrick hangs out a while, wanders back to the group and mingles for a while. As he's getting ready to leave, he comes back over to me.

"I'm gonna tell you something," he whispers, "but keep it between you and me. That baitfish they found in that pike, it *is* a herring. Been using them for bait a couple years now. Pike love 'em. End of the day, I drop 'em down the hole. Things sink right down to the bottom and stink to high hell—I think they keep the pike nearby."

A minor offense, I think to myself, the use of restricted bait. I am glad I've set up near Derrick's stink-trail.

"I won't tell a soul," I say.

Derrick reaches into his coveralls and pulls out a gallon zip-lock of half-thawed herring. "These things are pike candy," he says, offering me a glimpse. He smirks, then deftly slides the contraband back into its hiding place. "Seems like they're more interested in your live bait today, though," he says, firing up his four-wheeler and driving away.

By 2 p.m., everyone in the party has landed a pike. Some have landed their second. We are running out of bait.

Aaron and Ben walk out to another tripped flag with me, the rest engaged in a conversation about U.S. trade relations with China. At the trap, Aaron lands a juvenile pike, a "hammer-handle" in Maine vernacular, which bleeds heavily from its gills. We discard it on the ice for the eagles, then turn back toward camp, content with the fast fishing. Already it had been the best pike day I'd ever had, guiding or otherwise, and I think of how strange it is to enjoy the success with strangers who have never even fished before. As we walk, another flag pops between us and the shelter.

By the time we reach the hole, less than a minute after the tripper releases the flag, most of the spool's three hundred feet of line is gone. Ben hollers to the group, and this time they come running.

Derrick notices the commotion and beelines on his four-wheeler.

"This is a good one, Ben," I say, after he's set the hook and started the back-and-forth battle, the pike taking thirty or forty yards of line before conceding it. Derrick dismounts from his wheeler, kills the ignition, and walks to the hole.

"Want me to run that line for ya?" he asks.

I accept his offer and hand him the trap, while Ben pulls in line, piling it neatly on the ice. The rest of the group arrive, out of breath from the run. It is quite the scene—two Mainers and seven New Yorkers gathered around a hole punched in a frozen lake, brought together by this day of incredible fishing. I encourage Ben to keep pressure on the pike. The group watches intently. Aaron records video on his iPhone.

I kneel beside the hole, equal parts anxious and exhilarated. "Take your time," I tell Ben.

Three times I see the swivel connecting ice line to fluorocarbon leader, indicating that the fish is an arms-length away. Three times the pike flares at the sudden light from above. Fleeing line rubs Ben's fingers.

"Gee-zus," Derrick says, holding the tip-up to eye level, its silver spool surrendering line at an alarming rate. "She's runnin'!"

I cringe, hoping no one has heard him.

Ben gains back line. Finally, the pike stops beneath the hole, its head wide as the fat end of a bowling pin. Leader disappears into the corner of its mouth. When I reach my hand for the sweet spot, the pike twists violently, like an alligator. I keep my hand away from the teeth, dig again for the soft spot, and find it.

It's difficult to comprehend the sudden sight of such a fish, pulled from a dark lake, gasping and stunned. It's as if Messalonskee Lake has birthed something monstrous yet beautiful. I have forgotten my tape measure, which I always seem to do on days I need it, but the pike is clearly forty inches, if not longer. The guys laugh at the absurdity of their day, at the pike which seem progressively larger with each sprung flag.

"That's what twenty pounds looks like, boys," Derrick says, fist-bumping Ben, then me, happy to be part of the experience. Derrick knows, as I do, that a twenty-pound northern is a rare specimen, a once, or maybe twice-in-a-lifetime fish. I joke that we should pack it in; it isn't going to get any better.

I revive the pike by holding the fat ridge near its tail, keeping its head and body submerged. As it regains strength, its fin ripples against my bare wrist. The New Yorkers crowd around, with Derrick among them, all of us wanting to catch a last glimpse of the giant fish; all of sensing the end to this miraculous day, and perhaps sensing, too, the fleeting nature of our strange, serendipitous meeting.

When the fish tenses and curls its immense body, I release my grip. A swift tail kick, a boil settling in the hole, and the pike is gone.

LOST VOICES

When I learned that Tim Jackson, aka Jack, had
succumbed to cancer, I wanted to call him. Of course,
I realized my logical hiccup—no calls would be placed to the
dead—but still, it was my very first thought. I wanted to hear his
voice again.

"How they biting?" was how Jack answered my phone calls,
from when we first met in 2009, up until our last conversation,
over ten years later. Jack built high-end ice fishing traps. If you
met him at his shop, in Monmouth, Maine, I'm sure you heard
all about it. He liked to talk, especially about himself and his ice
fishing business. He branded his name onto his wooden tip-ups:
Tim Jack, he called himself, of Jack Traps, Inc.

Jack cold-called me first, having heard I was working on
a Maine ice fishing documentary. I needed to include him, he
insisted, since there couldn't really be a Maine ice fishing film
without him. I listened. Over the next decade I got to know
Jack from fishing with him, then from pointing a camera at
his overgrown beard, then from editing footage—raising and
lowering the levels of his booming voice—and, later, from our
infrequent phone calls.

It's hard to encapsulate a man with words, especially after
he's gone. There's a tendency to brush over complexity in an

effort to eulogize. To put it plainly, Jack seemed complicated. He was, in no particular order: a Mainer, businessman, husband, father, innovator, jokester, grump, occasional drinker, and salty, hardcore angler. Jack was a stranger to me, then a documentary subject, then friend, evolving finally into a loquacious, grizzly uncle-type I couldn't wait to fish with.

Jack lured me to East Grand Lake, on the Maine/New Brunswick border. I was filming what would become the documentary *Hardwater* and Jack had become one of the film's main characters. I remember his obsession with selecting the perfect East Grand bait (jumbo smelts only) and how he tended to them with the intensity of a child minding a beloved family pet. With his prized smelts we fished East Grand's deep hole, Jack's favorite fishing spot.

At dawn Jack plucked the best baits from the bucket and fed yards and yards of line down the hole with half-frozen fingers. If the hooked smelt didn't swim properly, if it fought against the downward drag of the line, he pulled it up and tried again—over and over, if necessary—until the bait swam just right to depths of 70, 80, 90 feet. It was agonizing to watch. But in those frigid moments, my own fingers numb against my camera, I realized I was watching a master.

When traps sprung, as they did frequently that morning, Jack reacted with a kind of cool confidence. Never rushing, he idled over on his four-wheeler before removing his oversize gloves. He walked slowly to the tip-up and peered down into the darkness—was the spool turning? If so, how fast? In which direction was the line pointing? When he was ready, which often took a while, Jack reached for the trap with his name branded on the crossbeam.

Without hyperbole, Tim Jackson was one of the greatest fishermen I've ever seen. He fought fish with a smooth, almost elegant hand-over-hand style, letting the big ones take line when necessary, never horsing them in. He was a bear of a man, so the thin ice fishing line looked absurd in his hands. When a hooked fish got close to the hole, Jack would kneel, as if proposing, and lift it gently from the frigid lake. *What's that saying?* he once asked the camera, holding up another fat lake trout. *Ten percent of fishermen catch 90 percent of the fish?*

If he sounded a bit arrogant, that's because he was—Jack knew he was good, and he wasn't shy about telling you so.

That morning, on East Grand Lake, while nearby anglers barely moved from their shacks, we landed lake trout from six to ten pounds. I had enough fish footage for five films. The largest specimen, a ten-pound lake trout, or *togue*, as Mainers call them, bled too much for proper release. Looking down at the dying togue, Jack said, with his trademark accent, *We'll have that bird for supper.*

Jack had a way of making me feel like I was one of the boys. He'd rib me if I missed a fish or congratulate me when I iced one. In the quiet moments between fish, Jack asked about my job, my love life, how the pike fishing was back on my home waters. If his arrogance was sometimes obvious, it took me a while to discover his deep sense of caring, since Jack shielded tenderness beneath his gruff exterior.

Jack was a natural storyteller, and through his stories I glimpsed his inner warmth. One story that resonated went something like this: When Jack was still too young to fish, his parents would bring home a live salmon after a day on the ice. Then they'd fill up the bathtub with cool water. Young Jack would get in the tub, and then his parents would drop in the fish. Jack recalled a large salmon, some fifty years prior, darting around his small, shivering body.

I wondered if that salmon sparked Jack's lifelong fascination with fish and fishing. I wonder now, thinking back, if making traps was Jack's way of preserving that salmon in the bathtub—to hold a transcendent memory that, like everything else, is eventually lost.

Cold winters I called Jack and his voice pulsed with life—good ice, product moving off the shelf faster than he and his team could keep up with. *Gotta get you up to East Grand again in early March, should be good!* Warm winters, Jack didn't have much to say, his voice flat and dejected. *Just no ice anywhere. I don't know anymore...* The trajectory of his trap-making business followed a kind of rollercoaster based on factors he could not control. I worried Jack was fighting a losing battle against warming, inconsistent winters.

In an effort to find *Hardwater's* ending, I asked characters to answer a few questions on camera. One of my questions was: If you died and came back as a fish, what would you be? I remember asking Jack that very question as we picked up for the day on East Grand, the weak March sun low in the sky, both of us buzzed on Crown Royal. Unlike the other film characters I'd asked, Jack didn't hesitate. *I know*, he said. *I know what I'd be. I've thought about this before.*

I double checked my camera's sound levels. In the fading afternoon light, I pointed the lens at Jack's bushy beard. *If I died and came back as a fish*, he said, *I'd be a togue. I'd be a big fat togue, just like I'm a big fat man. And I'd be good. I'd go around picking bait off of traps.*

During our last phone call, Jack invited me to Maranacook Lake. He'd dragged his shack out there, and he'd been making some good hauls on smelts early in the morning. He asked if I'd been working on any more films, and I told him I'd focused on writing instead. *Somebody, maybe you, ought to write a book*

Tim "Jack" Jackson with his ice auger.

about my life, Jack said. I chuckled, then realized he was dead serious. I politely declined, and the conversation shifted back to fishing. *Give me a call when you wanna come north*, he said, before wishing me well and hanging up. I'm not sure if Jack was sick then, but if so, he didn't mention it. I never followed up on his invitation.

The ways I'll remember Jack: ambling across East Grand with his auger slung over his shoulder. Auger-sprayed ice shards covering the tops of his green pack boots. His breath rising, hanging above his Mad Bomber hat. Reaching into the darkness to lift an impossibly large togue, its speckled flanks glistening in sunlight. The way his voice filled a room; the way his voice dissipated over the frozen expanse of East Grand Lake. The way he answered his cell phone: *How they biting?*

If a fish steals bait from one of my traps this winter, I won't feel disappointed. I'll grab another bait from the bucket, hook it gently beneath the dorsal fin, then drop it down into the darkness. I'll remind myself that it's probably just Jack paying a visit—voiceless, but not without humor—before swimming down to depths beyond my senses.

FOR LOVE OF HARDWATER

after Stephen Dunn

This time of year—mid-December—I love cold, still nights when temperatures plummet to single digits.

I love sitting by the woodstove and pulling old tip-ups from pack baskets. I love tying on fresh leaders, hooks right out of the package. I love the wooden clanks the traps make. I love a perfectly rigged trap with a button threaded so I can place bait exactly where I want. I love precision amidst our harshest season.

I love the efficiency of a good trap, how it trips again and again, how its beams display years in dents. I love how each one folds down into something smaller.

I love the first walk out, ice too thin for snowmobiles or four-wheelers. I love the shackless-lake. I love the quiet, the lack of auger sounds. I love the view through black ice, how if you look long enough the frozen air bubbles resemble stars in space. I love how I can walk on water, or through the night sky. I love how easily my heavy sled drags over glare ice. I love the bite of crampons with every step. I love the newness of it, love knowing this all will melt in a couple of months.

I love knowing there will be no jet-skis.

I love thinking of the fish's view—giant lid over their heads. I love imagining them watching the bottoms of my boots.

I love that first chisel into black ice. I love ice spray and the hollow thud right before I break through. I love how the lake seeps out, as if from a wound, how water pours and refreezes in uneven pools.

I love the visual confirmation of safety: three inches of clear black ice. I love standing atop cracks knowing I'm safe. I love the way water bobs in the chiseled holes the closer I walk.

I love that others love it, too.

I love walking single file, fifty feet apart from my friend, Jersey, whose real name is Steve; love that we both carry throw-bags, love that he doesn't mind when I remind him which state he's from. I love knowing we're prepared and hope we never need those preparations. I love knowing Jersey's summer job involves throwing rope to ejected rafters.

I love that he shows up early every time we fish. I love that Jersey skims holes and sets traps with steady diligence. I love how he takes FaceTime calls from his young son, shows him the trap he's resetting. I love his optimism.

More than the tripped trap, I love the moment before, the flag held down by the tiny O-ring. I love the simple physics, the harnessed potential. I love the shape of the set trap, too, like half a heart.

I love the moment of recognition: *Flag*!

I love the way, once called, that word punctuates everything else: meals, conversations, it doesn't matter. I love the possibilities the word contains. I love yelling it, but I love hearing it yelled just as much.

I love the way the flag hovers, a cloth beacon of hope. I love running, the way Jersey and I run, to the first tripped traps of the new year. I love being out of breath in winter clothes. I love how heavy my boots feel those last few yards.

I love the moment before I see the spool. I love the way my mind turns, in that moment.

I love the spool-blur only big fish produce.

I love the direct connection—no rod, no reel. I love the headshakes, the long, finger-burning runs.

I love lifting fish from the darkness. I love releasing fish, and I love keeping a few white perch for dinner—pan seared, with a squeeze of lemon juice.

I love the simplicity of jig poles.

I love that salmon hunt just beneath the ice. I love that pike piss off the purists.

I love that in the first photo of me fishing I'm sitting on the floor of Dad's ice shack with my hand stuck in a Cheez-It's box.

I love that I only see certain people on the ice, year after year, though I know they live nearby all year round.

I love how voices carry over ice.

I love skillet-seared venison on a Coleman stove.

I love bald eagles waiting for discarded baits.

I love fishless days because we were out there trying.

I love getting into bed, after. I love how quickly I fall asleep, how I wake not having moved all night.

I love the recurring dream I've had since I was a boy: ice fishing over an impossibly gnarled tree, which I can see somehow in cross-section, me trying to pull in a fish that's wrapped itself among the limbs. I love how I always consider diving in but wake before I have the chance. I love knowing I might have another opportunity.

I love the coyote that watched me on Messalonskee Lake. I love that I woke from my nap just as it passed, silently, loved that I wasn't dreaming at all.

I love the groans lakes make in February, because I'm tired of winter then, too.

I love that Mainers call lake trout *togue*.

I love footwarmers that last till 4 p.m.

I love fishing warm March days in a t-shirt.

I love how many weather systems one winter's day contains.

I love how most of the time nothing much happens. I love how one flag flying changes everything.

I love that I'll meet up with Jersey in a couple of weeks if cold weather holds.

I love that he'll get there before me, will have already gathered his traps and chisel lakeside. I love that I'll spot him by the light of his headlamp.

I love that we'll fall in line: one of us chiseling, checking ice thickness, the other dragging a sled full of traps, bait, food. I love that the lake will hold us.

I love that one of us will set the year's first trap, and one of us will spot the first flag.

I love that we'll drop whatever we're doing, in that moment—and run.

FALSE CASTS

On my third cast I unfurl a perfect eighty-foot shot, leader landing soft as a snowflake a few feet from the tarpon's nose. A few bumps and the fish lunges forward, inhaling my homemade fly. It turns in a silver flash, and I set, feeling its weight like I'm hitched to a train car. Fly line surges and it's airborne: gills rattling, frothing ocean, then jumping again, line bouncing off the deck. Clear to the reel, handle melting to a blur.

"Catch anything?" says a man from behind me. I turn just in time to see his labradoodle squat beside the walking path.

I force a smile. "Nothing yet," imagining the satisfaction of strip-setting a 2/0 fly in his pooch's tail. "But I've got a good feeling about this spot."

Of course, I'm not standing on the front of a skiff casting across turquoise flats into a light tropical breeze. My eyes aren't strained from staring through the glare, searching for silhouettes. Instead, I'm in the middle of a snowed-over Eastern Promenade, dead-legged in oversize pack boots, casting a brittle twelve-weight at fallen tree limbs. It's January, Maine, a light snow falling, the sky low and slate gray. The only migration going on here is a steady stream of ski-bums slinking north to Sugarloaf.

The man with the dog chuckles. "Big fly rod you got there. Tarpon?"

"Good guess. You fish for them?"

"I caught one way back in the '80s, a smaller one," he says. "Belize. Amazing fish."

"They sure are," I say. "I'm obsessed."

"I can see that," he says, then wishes me luck and continues walking.

Parker shows up ten minutes later, parking his truck behind mine and ambling over the snowbank in his work clothes.

"You're crazy, you know that right?" he says.

"I'm aware," I say. "But you're here too, so I'm not sure what that says about you."

He's met me for some winter casting, which we're aiming to do once a week, regardless of weather. He has some work to do. We've scheduled a week-long Keys trip together for early May. The plan is to tow my seventeen-foot Ranger Ghost and rent an AirBnB, in Islamorada, with a private boat launch. I'm hoping to connect Parker with his first tarpon. He's not there yet with his fly rod skills, but practice should get him closer, or so I'm hoping.

I'm not trying to wish winter away, a season I love, but it's heartening to imagine our trip south together. The biting northwest wind numbs my fingers. The sky is gray and heavy and I haven't felt sunlight, truly warm rays, in three or four months. Parker takes the twelve-weight and makes some false casts. He's been working on his bad habits, which still show themselves until he warms up, until he gets in rhythm. His loop crumbles because he's forcing it, not letting the rod do its work. Fly line piles and slides across the snow.

I'm no expert, but years of fishing and casting lessons and some degree of obsessiveness (inherited from Dad, I'm sure) have me dialed in with efficient, accurate casting. Fishing the Keys helps, too—there's no more challenging fishery within a day's travel. If you can't cast down there you're done before you begin. I encourage Parker to open his back cast and stop his rod tip sooner, so he can shoot the line before his spin fishing habits betray him.

Parker takes criticism without bristling and adjusts as best he can. He wants to get better, which is why he's out here in January, after a long workday, warming his hands in between casts. I wish he'd practice more on his own, and sometimes I worry I'm pushing him toward goals he's not invested in, like trying to jump a tarpon on a fly rod. He seems just as content chucking lures or bait, but I know how that first airborne tarpon, shaking its head to get rid of the fly, can immediately change an angler's life.

A few years back I made the mistake of bringing Parker along on a guided tarpon trip with Rich. The wind was ripping twenty-five miles per hour from the southeast, the bay water chilly. The weather pattern had hung around, making fishing more than difficult. Rich was in a mood as foul as the weather. The first day, Parker had a couple shots at backcountry tarpon, one of which was forty feet off the bow, a layup, as they say, but Parker's cast was short. The wind knocked down his attempts, which were tentative. Rich, poling his ass off to keep him positioned in the wind, lost patience with Parker, told him he looked like he was waving a magic wand. He kept on him, his own frustration seeping out at Parker's poor casting. Coming to Parker's defense, I lost my patience with Rich and the skiff went quiet.

We worked it out afterwards, but I felt badly for throwing Parker into the fire before he was ready. It reminded me of the first time I'd brought him fishing to the trout spot, except tarpon fishing was even tougher.

But he didn't seem to mind. Parker took Rich's criticism better than I did, which impressed me. Later that same day, tucked behind a mangrove islet to get out of the gale, Rich spotted a massive pink-backed tarpon, floating at the surface, trying to warm up.

"Parker, you ready for another shot?" he asked. His question seemed to smooth everything over immediately, and the tension left the skiff. Parker didn't hesitate.

And he made a good cast, landed the fly softly just right of the massive fish, probably 150 pounds, but it didn't take. Still, it was a good shot at the sleeping giant. I watched Parker perk up with confidence.

We fished with Rich again, a few years after—a successful, perfect-weather trip in which Parker landed a big snook and redfish. It said a lot about his character, getting back on Rich's skiff and holding his head high.

And this coming May, it'll be me on the poling platform, on my own boat, and I'm hoping that will take some of the pressure off. I want Parker to launch a tarpon in the worst way.

I barely notice strange looks from passers-by as we rearrange branches at various fish-like angles in the snow: a few drivers slow and rubberneck as Parker casts. Others walk by as if nothing is out of the ordinary, just two grown men fly fishing in a frozen field. I pace off fifty yards and Parker casts at me, his loops tighter and aim truer.

A fly cast is, in a sense, a distillation of the angler. There, in Parker's rushed fore-stroke, the muscle memory of spin fishing for stripers, launching heavy plugs into the surf. Parker's back cast unfurls, loop opening too far, then he shifts his feet and shoots the line forward, snapping at the end to stop the tip's momentum. It's not a beautiful cast by any means, but he gets it out there. I grab the fly-less leader and Parker practices two-handing the line, like he's fishing a worm fly on the ocean, which he will be doing before too long. I walk toward him slowly, leader in hand. I want him to feel what it's like when a tarpon takes his fly, though nothing can prepare you for the real thing. I stop. Parker strips and line tightens. He smirks and sets the imaginary hook, too gently.

"Try again, like you mean it."

He casts again, I grab the leader, stop, line tightens, and this time he nearly rips the leader from my hand. I pull line from the reel. Parker is hunched over, breathing heavily, pulling as hard as he can.

"Two hundred pounds of dead weight," I say.

"It's not so bad," Parker grunts.

"Not bad? You look like you're gonna pass out. It's been thirty seconds—imagine fifty minutes."

"Maybe I'll jump one and break it off," he says.

It's another four months before Parker's next shot at *Megalops*. We'll drift crabs at night and fly fish by day, weather permitting. And yet, this weekend we'll pass the time ice fishing, setting wooden traps with cold-clumsy fingers. Augers and snow machines and shanties. Nothing further from the flats.

We talk a while about our upcoming drive, plan to map out our best route. Parker drives a lot for his work, managing a stormwater treatment team, so he's good at finding routes and making long pushes on the road. He suggests we leave late evening, so we'll run the northeast gauntlet at night, after rush hour, with the least amount of traffic, minimizing the potential hazards while trailing a boat. It's a good idea. It's daunting, the prospect of driving 27 hours, the stress of staring in the rearview at a skiff, one sideswipe or snoozing trucker away from disaster. I'm glad Parker will be there, and we'll take turns driving, not pushing it. We'll rest when necessary, or so we tell ourselves, though we both know the pull of the flats, the prospect of tarpon fishing, will get us those last hundred miles regardless of our fatigue.

It's getting late, and I haven't regained feeling in my hands. Parker reels in line and hands me the fly rod. We head to our trucks, stomping snow from our boots when we make it to the road. I break down the fly rod and stow it in its case. We plan to cast again next week, maybe on a warmer day.

Parker unlocks his truck, opens the driver's side door.

"Is it May yet? he asks.

"Not quite yet," I say.

BOUNDARY LINES

At dawn we idle through mangrove tunnels and emerge in Florida Bay. Disturbed by our approach, mullet dimple the glassy surface. Smells of tidal rot and fish hang on the air. Above, pelicans glide in loose formation. The temperature—hovering in the low seventies—feels incredible after the Maine winter I've endured.

Rich sits next to me at the wheel of his Whipray, bundled in a thick Simms coat, his sun mask pulled up for warmth. I suppose this is chilly, as far as Keys' weather is concerned, but I'm content in my t-shirt and shorts.

"I have an extra coat if you want it," Rich says.

"This is the warmest I've been in five months. I think you're getting a little soft."

"Oh, for sure!" he says, laughing.

Channel markers blink red, green. Mangrove islets loom on the horizon. Rich navigates narrow channels and shallow hummocks until we're running, really cruising now, past Lignumvitae Key, headed northwest toward the boundary of Everglades National Park.

Rich leans my way and talks over the outboard. "Everyone's tarpon fishing, even though the water's still too cold," he says.

"Calm days like this, early in the season, backcountry fishing can be on fire."

By backcountry fishing, Rich means redfish, sea trout, and snook, sight-fished in shallow water. I've booked two days hoping for tarpon, in this our fifth year fishing together. I've learned that we can't force it. We can't change the weather, and rather than beating our heads against a wall trying to tempt a grumpy, too-cold tarpon, we can pivot toward the backcountry, which feels like another universe.

I trust Rich's judgement. Now that we've landed several tarpon together, the pressure I'd felt to land one on a fly has dissipated. I've grown to trust Rich entirely, to synch up with his method of taking what each day offers. Rich admits he doesn't have a clear plan for each day; instead, he uses his intuition, his senses, his backlog of information, and, once we're on the water, he prefers to let the steering wheel take us in the right direction.

Ahead, cormorants flap in awkward take-off; we nearly overtake one, before it veers. Rich steers through channels and over unseen hazards he's memorized over the years, buzzes past flats where egrets and herons and spoonbills stand still as statues. The bay mirrors a purpled sky. Behind us, the immense Florida sun noses over the horizon. A few other skiffs—guides with clients, I figure—scatter north and south, sticking close to town.

"Not a bad commute," Rich says loudly, and I nod, wishing I could slow this all down, or return to the moment, somehow, once I'm back home.

A half hour later, far from the chaos of Route 1 traffic, Rich takes the Whipray off plane and we glide toward a shallow grass flat, deep in the backcountry. Why he chose here is beyond me, but I'm not questioning his decision.

Clouds have followed us. Rich gets up on the platform but can't see anything, since the clouds obscure our vision into the shallows. He stakes out and we eat breakfast: cold pizza from the night before, a night out in Key Largo with Rich and his guide-buddy, Chris, who is guiding for bonefish today.

"Let's just be patient," Rich says. "See what happens."

We are finishing up the cold pizza—ricotta and sausage on thin crust, nearly as good as it had been the night before—when Rich perks up.

"Look over there, two o'clock."

A long cast away, a redfish tail blades the surface.

"That's what happens when you let Mother Nature do her thing," Rich says. He climbs the platform. I wipe pizza grease on my sun pants and grab the nine weight.

I inspect the fly: a shrimpy creation with bead-chain eyes and minimal flash. Rich, who knows I am a fly tyer but also someone to trust with his favorite patterns, Rich who sees everything, it seems, says, "That fly is redfish candy. Just let him see it."

High clouds create serious glare, but I can make out the body of the feeding redfish. I wait for it to glide out of its tipped feeding position and then make my cast.

"Didn't see it, go again," Rich says.

This time, the fly lands perfectly ahead of the redfish. It rushes and inhales my fly, gills flared. It's a good fight, and a solid red for backcountry Florida. Rich removes the fly, we bump fists, and then we're fishing again.

"See, all we gotta do is sit and eat and something good will happen," he jokes. "I'll be known as the guide who stakes out and eats pizza."

The clouds break up, and I can see the shallow sand pockets—little craters—amidst various brown-olive matts of seagrass.

It's hard to differentiate boundaries out here: seafloor, surface, sky, all touching or reflecting one another, shifting with the shifting light, clouds scudding, obscuring our view, then passing, everything lit up again. There is no clear horizon line; the bay melts and shimmers into the skyline, and on that strange horizontal plane wading birds stand, shifting and blurring as they walk, as if part of some vast backcountry mirage.

We spot a few mud-puffs, telltale signs of spooked snook.

"Those fuckers are so hard to see," Rich says, without introduction, and it's clear to me we are on the same wavelength. We're gliding in a foot of water.

The first snook we spot hovers over a sand hole parallel to another, its mirror image almost, and, when I drop the fly a foot off their noses, the current sweeps it perfectly toward them. The fish nearest me, the larger one, stalks the fly, which disappears into its mouth.

"Got him!" Rich says. "That's a *beast!*"

Certain guide slang, I've learned, describes unusually large or special fish efficiently: *beast*, for example, or *moose*, or *giant*. Rich's description of the snook fastened to the end of my line has my heart rate spiked. I'm into the backing.

Rich poles after it because starting the motor would spook everything in the zip code. I gain line, then the snook runs. This back-and-forth pattern continues for a while, before I manage to get the snook within range.

"Go easy this last bit," Rich said, "They'll wear right through that thirty-pound." I can tell by the timbre of his voice that he's nervous.

Rich stakes the pole and descends the platform, then readies himself at the gunwale. I lead the tired snook to him. My view of the grab is blocked but I can hear the fish's final protest, splashing Rich as he secures it, two-handed, by its giant mouth. He lifts it into the skiff.

"What a snook!" he says. He's as excited as I've ever seen him.

We take photos quickly, anxious to get the snook back in the water. Its black lateral line resembles the brush stroke of a monochrome ink painting. Its girth is impressive, thick from gills to tail. Rich revives it carefully. I can sense his reverence for the fish, even more so than for the big tarpon we've landed together. The snook kicks off out of sight.

"You don't see many like that one," Rich says, tying on a fresh leader and fly. I thank him for the push, the set-up.

Getting back on the casting platform after such a moment is a test of one's attention—lingering in success is seductive but distracts from the next opportunity, from what's coming that we can't yet see. Rich is calling out another fish up ahead.

"Solo snook, sand hole at one, see him?"

Rich releasing a healthy backcountry snook.

I do. My cast is on the money. The snook charges and eats.

I let out a holler. Rich shouts. It's nearly the same size as the last one, and it wears the leader to a frayed strand, but we land it. Our day is beyond made.

After we release the snook, I say, "Get up front and take some shots," expecting Rich to refuse.

"Alright," he says, "if you say so."

I've never been on the back of his skiff before. Rich doesn't need much help—not with his hawk-eyes and years of experience fishing here. But still, it's nice to push the skiff a while, to watch him fish instead of being watched. It's nice to be trusted with the task.

Rich spots a redfish before I do and casts over its back, a low percentage shot, but the fish turns and eats.

I land the redfish for him, a complete role reversal, then take a picture with the redfish draped over his lap.

"Been a while since I've been on the pointy end," Rich says, thanking me, and I feel the deep satisfaction that comes when you witness someone doing something they love, something they don't often get to do. We've been fishing three hours and have already caught specimens that would win most backcountry fly tournaments. Rich poles for a while longer, but we don't spot anything.

"Let's head back toward town," Rich says. "Water temps should be climbing," which has me excited again, since he's referencing tarpon without naming them.

I rinse off the redfish slime and stow the nine weight. Rich checks his phone and I get water from the hatch. We sit and drink them down, in the heart of the backcountry. The light is bright white and disorienting, and even through my polarized lenses the bay looks overexposed.

I know I'll get a few tarpon shots—they're bound to be floating around town, taking in the warm afternoon sun—but I'm still thinking about snook, about their black stripe, about the blurred boundaries out here in the backcountry.

I do catch a big tarpon near town, but that's another story for another time. We drink Modelo back at the dock and make plans for the next morning, my mind stuck on the snook in the skinny water. I think of the birds standing on the horizon where bay meets sky, as if they might fall off into another dimension, and how fish and birds and seascapes borrow from one another, or blend somehow, I'm not exactly sure, the beer doing quick work to my already zapped brain. I need a shower, a nap, a dark room with air conditioning.

After some water and time to regain my composure, we head to the marina's parking lot, where we make plans for dinner. Rich rinses the Whipray. It's the color of Maine snow in late March—off-white, almost gray. Soon I'll be back home, snow blanketing the frozen ground, lakes still ice capped, spring close on the calendar but still feeling like an impossibility. It's hard to imagine this is the same country—Maine in March, and here, the Florida Keys, and the shifting light of the flats. It's hard to imagine that the road I'll soon turn onto—Route 1—could take me all the way home, though that would take a while; could take me past home, even, on up to Aroostook County, with its moose and muskies and friendly locals with strange hybrid accents.

I walk to my rental car. A green iguana shimmies over sun-bleached stones.

A POLE DOWN
MEMORY LANE

The old man leaves the marina early, though he knows he'll find no competition where he's headed. The few guides that remain—too young to remember him in his prime—wait for clients, decide who will stake out where, along the oceanside. He idles past, into a gauntlet of mangroves. When he's out of sight, one of the guides says: "You see that? Not a rod in his boat. Must be off for a pole down memory lane!"

The chug of his engine muffles their laughter. The mangrove tunnel widens, and Florida Bay opens before him. Small purple isles shimmer on the horizon. How many times had he made this run? He's not sure. He buries the throttle. The skiff planes, slashes the sky's mirror.

It's been years, but he still remembers the route. The landmarks look the same: wooden stakes bent like hockey sticks along a bank where cormorants rested with outstretched wings; a deep, narrow channel between mangrove islands, his sure-bet snook spot; the bonefish flat where tailers pushed into the tide. This morning, everything is still. No V-wakes, no birds.

Behind him, the enormous sun pushes into the sky, but the air is still cool upon his face. He knows he's getting close, would sense it blindfolded. He smells the sweet rotting stink of the backcountry, but there's a new scent, too, vaguely chemical, upon the air. To the northeast, he spots the abandoned buildings of Flamingo.

He takes the skiff off plane, eases the throttle back, kills the ignition. In the new silence he unfastens the push pole, carries it to the stern, climbs the platform. He stands and steadies himself.

His heart sinks when his push-pole finds sludge. What had he expected? Certainly not to hear it crunch through healthy turtle grass that once stretched for acres, here? Certainly not to peer down through water clear as mountain air and watch blue crabs scuttle for cover, grass shrimp pulse with other-worldly translucence, wings of spotted rays flap silently from beneath his bow?

He poles farther into the lake, one of the myriad lakes where tarpon rested, fed, daisy-chained, free-jumped. His beloved tarpon. He had been a nut for them, had often dreamt and still did dream of their prismatic scales and slow, upward strikes and the sounds they made in brief flight. This had been his favorite spot of all.

The water is reddish-brown now, foam-slicked, foreign. He's grateful for his sun mask, which reduces the stench.

He closes his eyes, tries to remember. When he opens them, something miraculous happens.

On the bow is his favorite client, Danny, dead ten years now, wearing the same ridiculous floral t-shirt he always wore. The old man is so startled by his apparent hallucination that he dares not blink for fear of breaking the spell. When he looks out, the lake is as it once was: clear as crystal, and alive. A big, brown-backed tarpon rolls. It is as if he is watching an old film but also participating in it, somehow.

"Roller at one o'clock, did you see her?" he asks.

"Sure did," Danny says.

He swings the bow and poles closer and the fish rolls again, sixty feet out.

"Go ahead."

Danny makes the shot. The fly lands softly. He watches his good friend make a long, sure-handed strip and then the tarpon is airborne; the old man's heart soars with it.

When the tarpon crashes down he blinks and is alone again.

He looks at his hands and finds sun spots, wrinkles. The air stinks, the lake covered in red slime. He blinks, tries to summon the dream—to re-enter it—but he is stuck helplessly in the present.

What could he have done differently? he wonders. He had signed petitions, organized rallies in Tallahassee, joined other guides, raised his voice. The politicians had all said, "Yes, we'll make this our priority!" They hadn't. It was too late now.

There was a time when sweet water nourished the Everglades, and tarpon rolled over backcountry turtle grass flats. It is too painful to remember. Nostalgia is useless, he thinks, as virulent as algae.

He realizes he's forgotten his own water. How could that be? The sun is high and hot, his throat sandpaper. He won't last long. He descends the platform, fastens the pole, fires the ignition.

Turning for home, he imagines cold, clean water upon his tongue.

SOUNDS OF SPRING

Dad doesn't hear well anymore, even with his hearing aids cranked. On the phone I get frustrated when he talks over me, or when there's a long pause after I've shared something important. "Dad, can you hear what I'm saying?" I ask, not hiding my irritation.

"Not really," he says, and then I try again, only louder. If I'm in a decent mood, I laugh it off, and Dad laughs along with me.

It's helpful to remember his hearing loss is normal for a 78-year-old, a man who regularly fired rifles and shotguns for decades. It's helpful to remember that he can still decipher some tones better than others: a twig snapping beneath an approaching buck, for example, more so than my low, soft voice.

I should mention he's musically tone deaf—in fact, I think my entire family is tone deaf, myself included. That said, I carry a tune better than my father can, which has helped me in the more musical aspects of turkey hunting.

Which is to say: when we turkey hunt together, my father and I, I am the designated caller. That's because operating a box call takes some degree of rhythm, some recognition of pitch and tone and projection. I'm the best chance we've got.

I've tried to teach my father techniques for subtle, quiet calls, the ones that seal the deal in bringing big, wary toms those last few necessary yards. It hasn't gone well.

Box calls are meant to sound raspy—like a hen that's dying to meet a big, long-bearded tom. My dad's call sounds, well, like a hen that's simply dying, or choking on a corn kernel, or screeching for help as it's strangled by a fox.

What's more alarming is that he has—on numerous occasions—called in and shot toms while hunting alone, which speaks perhaps more to those particular toms' mating inclinations than it does my father's calling.

Once, about fifteen years ago, my father and I, both novice turkey hunters, set up hen decoys on the edge of a green field in Mercer. I remember the pine bark I rested against, and my father to my right against another tree; him with the shotgun, me with the box call. Turkey hunting is best first thing in the morning, and so we set up long before shooting light. I don't remember hearing much of anything, just the occasional drone of eighteen-wheelers along Route 2. I remember daylight slowly lifting and the greening field and my eyes itching from pollen, and the feeling that nothing much was going to happen.

I remember the boughs above us swooshing in the wind, and a few crows riding the updrafts. I remember my calling: soft notes at first, then louder. I didn't really know what I was doing, and my calls didn't elicit responses, which did not surprise me.

By 8 a.m., I had grown restless and hungry. I swatted mosquitoes. My father watched the field intently. A few minutes later he leaned and whispered: "Try a few more calls. We'll give it a half hour. If nothing happens, we'll get out of here."

I nodded. Relieved at having a plan, I fantasized about breakfast. I waited a few moments, then let off a series of low purrs with the box call, gradually raising the volume. I finished the series with a few loud, ear-ringing shrieks.

Immediately, a gobble from far off. My dad pointed in the general direction: "Did you hear that?" he whispered. I nodded again.

One of the hardest components of turkey hunting is knowing when to call, and when to shut up. You want to keep the tom's attention, but you don't want to overdo it by calling too much.

I called once more—a series of two or three raspy vocalizations to which there were no responses.

We waited. Sweat rolled down my back. My stomach rumbled. Fifteen minutes, a half hour. Nothing. The wind picked up. My father and I looked at each other. He shrugged.

I'm not sure why we waited longer. There was no logical reason to do so: I heard nothing but the wind in the trees, and my growling stomach. My body ached from sitting still so long.

And that's when I saw it: the big tom's head as he approached along the field edge, left to right.

If you think dinosaurs don't exist, you've never watched a tom's red-blue head bob through trees like a small-scale velociraptor. My father saw it, too. He raised his shotgun and rested it on his knees.

The tom was still out of range, and every few feet it slowed to survey the field. When it got to about sixty yards, it stopped completely, fanned, then spun like a top. It wouldn't come any closer.

I waited and watched. The tom stood frozen. I scratched out a few soft clucks, barely audible, trying to recapture his attention.

It worked. In he came: full trot, head up, steady march toward our decoys, silent, no gobbling. I heard the *click* of Dad's safety.

When you fire at clay pigeons above a September field your ears trap the sound. When you fire your .308 at a target in late October the crack goes through your bones. When your father fires his twelve gauge at a giant tom you've called in in the first week of May, you hear nothing.

The tom is strutting, black iridescence with a red-blue head and then he's down, feathers rustling, spurs kicking the sky. There's only silence, and Dad's look of disbelief, and my own mind trying to make sense of this impossibility made suddenly possible, made into reality, and the sound of my body moving again—loosening—reaching down and lifting the tom's heft.

"Look at the size of that thing!" Dad said. "He came in so quietly, he was just *there* all of a sudden! He liked those soft calls. Couldn't resist."

My father took a photo of me walking out of the field that morning, twenty-one pounds of turkey slung over my shoulder. He framed it for me a few years ago, and I keep the frame in my apartment.

Photographs like this one exist in one dimension: me in camo, back to frame, giant bird on my back. But still— somehow—the sounds remain within the photograph: pine boughs, father's whisper, box call, gobble, safety click. I hear them all in memory. I like to retrieve them this time of year when the fields start to green. I hear the sounds, over and over. I know my father hears them too, hears them even though he can't hear my voice well anymore.

Spring is for tarpon and turkey hunting.

PAIR OF JACKS

I was anchored at the edge of a shallow, hard-bottom flat near Craig Key, staring down-light as the afternoon tide swept in. An easterly breeze kicked the stern in the direction fish would come from, which was less than ideal, but I was fishing alone and had no say in the matter. I climbed the poling platform of the shitty rental boat and scanned the flat: June sunlight played off greens and browns of the turtle grass and sand-pocked bottom. A bonnethead shark patrolled the shallows. I thought briefly of throwing to it, but figured my small, ginger-colored shrimp fly wouldn't get its attention or, if it did, I might lose the fly altogether.

I scanned beyond the shark—back toward land—Route 1 only a few long casts away, and saw a large tarpon gliding toward me at a perfect angle. It followed the edge of the flat as though it were a walking trail and the fish a pedestrian, instead of the hundred-pound behemoth it appeared to be. I cast. My fly landed a little far, slightly across its path. I waited until the tarpon was within a few feet of the fly, which looked absurd and tiny when I slid it. For a moment I thought the fish might follow, but it kept to the contour of the flat. I re-cast and the tarpon sensed me and twitched like a horse trying to rid a fly from its flank. It crossed the grass and disappeared.

The tarpon must have seen me from a long way off, all six-foot-five of me standing atop the platform waving a nine-foot rod. How many flies had been plunked in its path during its long lifetime? I was feeling a little sorry for the fish, and for myself, when I saw what appeared to be two jacks approaching from dead down-light.

I'd seen schools of jacks here before—ten to twenty fish, terrorizing the flat—but never just two. They came into range at breakneck pace. I stripped in line and launched a fifty-foot back cast, which—as casts often go when an angler only has time to react—landed perfectly. I bumped the fly once, twice, and the trailing fish accelerated. At forty-five feet I saw white, rubbery lips, a slash of yellow as it flashed and ate, and realized I'd cast not to a pair of jacks, but to two large permit.

It hoovered my fly as if it were starving, and then my brain malfunctioned. Call it a faulty electrical impulse, blame it on overactive reflexes. Before the permit closed its mouth, I strip-set. My fly bounced off its lips, my line slackened. The permit startled, swam in wild, angry loops, then bolted, along with its comrade, at around the speed of light.

I just stood there. My tarpon fly, which had spent a millisecond inside a permit's cheek, sank to bottom, fixed absurdly to sixty-pound shock tippet. I made no attempt to retrieve it. The tide kept coming in. I thought of a friend who'd endured four permit-less trips to Belize without so much as a lean. I thought of McGuane, whose first permit came to hand, after so many failures, on a tarpon fly. I thought of whom to call—Rich, Parker, Dad—those who might most appreciate my story, those who could console me. I stripped in line. My fly was one-eyed, my only evidence of the brief contact with what would have been my first permit on a fly. I decided not to call anyone. I'd write about it, I told myself, once the pain wore off.

THE CAST

I met Parker in the parking lot of the Biddeford Walmart. It was drizzling, late April, and I'd just finished my last day of teaching for the semester. I'd ended classes a week early so we could drive to the Keys together. I wanted to get him his first tarpon.

We'd booked an AirBnB ground floor apartment for a week, bayside in Tavernier, with its own private boat launch, A/C, a small but functional kitchen, two beds. The Ranger Ghost was hitched to Parker's dad's truck, and we'd paid him for the wear and tear it was about to experience. My truck was too old, and I worried it would break down or blow a tire somewhere along the way.

I'd zip-tied the nineteen-foot push pole so it didn't become a free flying javelin among 95-South traffic. Parker's fiancé, Cait, dropped him off, and they shuttled Parker's many bags into the truck, along with his fly rod cases, lure and fly boxes. I could tell he had too much shit, which was not unusual, but he'd also brought giant Ziplock bags of trail mix and other assorted snacks, so I forgave him. Cait told us to drive safely and stay in touch, and I assured her we would. As I merged onto the highway, Parker said, "We there yet?"

The first few hours were uneventful, despite the steady rain falling—I was jacked up on adrenaline, and all I could think of was a week of limitless fishing, of Parker launching his first tarpon. Our plan—one we had agreed upon after negotiation, since Parker's tendency was to push long distance driving, while mine was to break it up—was that neither of us would drive more than four hours at a time. The GPS on the dash said we'd arrive in Tavernier in just under twenty-seven hours.

Near Lowell, Massachusetts, the rain started pouring down. For the next two hours I white knuckled behind, beside, between eighteen-wheelers, smear of brake lights reddening the dash. Parker stayed awake, told me how he was overworked because his company was short-staffed, and after a while I had a hard time paying attention to the road and his story. We gassed up in Connecticut, rain pelting the asphalt.

Around midnight we made it to the Mario Cuomo Bridge, crossed over into New Jersey and tucked onto the Palisades Parkway, even though trailers weren't allowed. My brain was mush and I needed rest, and I had tired of the Chex Mix batch that had the cab reeking of stale garlic powder. I pulled into a rest stop on the Jersey Turnpike and Parker jammed into the backseat. I laid across the front seats and closed my eyes. The whooshing sounds of eighteen-wheelers made sleep impossible, as did the general anxiety of parking my skiff in a sketchy, poorly lit Jersey truck stop at one in the morning.

After twenty minutes trying and failing to sleep we pushed on, Parker's turn to drive, and I dozed periodically, startling awake to strange thoughts or the sensation that we were drifting off the highway.

Petty blared as we cruised through pre-dawn Washington, D.C., no other vehicles on the road. It was my shift behind the wheel. Fluorescent lights of the too-narrow Chesapeake Tunnel. Trail mix. So much trail mix. Parker fielding calls from his fiancé:

"We're in Virginia."

"Yes, still driving."

"It's fine, we're taking turns."

"Call you when we get there."

Skiff in the rearview: seventeen-footer my father helped me buy. Tire pressure checks. Largest Confederate flag I'd ever seen, flying above the highway, in South Carolina. Georgia Waffle House with A/C set to freeze-your-ass-off, greasy bacon, fake eggs. Welcome to Florida! sign, and the GPS showing seven more hours to go.

I remember how well I slept that first night, the hum of the air conditioner in our rental apartment, in Tavernier, not far from where Rich lived. I remember exploring the big back yard and private boat ramp in the morning, which was a small sandy strip where we'd left the skiff, rigged for the week of fishing. Florida Bay beyond, shimmering pink-purple-orange in the early light. It felt like waking into a dream that was better than any dream I'd had in sleep.

And already it was Friday morning, our last day. Something about tarpon fishing has always warped time and space; it couldn't be Friday, but it was. We'd had mixed-bag weather, with moderate winds and decent light and a few thunderstorms that chased us off the water. We'd each landed a tarpon on conventional gear, including Parker's first, which he'd caught on a live crab at night, a thirty-minute battle that left his forearms seizing. It was fun to watch Parker struggling with a fish that weighed about the same as him. I had grabbed the fish boatside and could not get my arm around it as I tried to right it in the current.

Fly fishing, though, had been beyond tough, and neither of us had hooked a tarpon. I was trying to come to peace with it, to appreciate the time we'd had, to accept that it was not Parker's time yet. If anything, those cold hours casting on the Promenade had toughened us, brought us closer together, had given us structure and camaraderie with which to navigate the toughest season.

Eggs and sausage on a hot plate, toast, orange juice. I applied sunscreen, threw on my stinky sun shirt and shorts. Parker scrolled on his phone on the couch. He got himself moving, stretched out his boat-back, took a shot of water and rubbed sunscreen on his ears and nose. We launched the skiff.

Ominous clouds had built to the east like a grayscale skyline. I poled bayside with Parker on the bow; then lightning nearby and the thought that holding a nineteen-foot composite pole, atop an elevated platform with water all around might not be the safest scenario. We raced in before the storm, but the storm caught us and drenched us. I beached the skiff and we ran in over the Bermuda grass, back to the apartment.

We sat on the couch, scrolled through weather apps with waning optimism, the brightly colored radar washing out hope for last-minute fly fishing. Parker was grateful to have landed one on conventional gear. He had kept a palm-sized scale to mark the occasion. This was the Florida Keys, after all, and rain and storms were to be expected. Still, I felt a little cheated. I felt guilty saying it aloud, but I knew Parker felt it, too, was too polite to say anything about disappointment. An hour went by, rain hammered the roof, and we both went to our respective rooms to change, and pack.

When you've driven 1,642 miles dragging a skiff and you're
faced with those same 1,642 miles, in reverse, one week later,
your mind wobbles. I tried not to think about it and failed.
Our plan was to catch a few hours' sleep and leave for Maine
around midnight. We finished packing and stowed our bags in
the hallway. We put leftovers into plastic bags for the road, took
stock of our dwindling water supply. I brought my bags out to
the truck.

A rainbow arched over the bay, and beyond, a line of lighter
clouds. Rain had shifted to drizzle, and winds eased. Parker came
out hauling his heaviest bag. He checked out the sky and we
looked at each other with *Well, what do you think?* expressions.

Within five minutes we were back on the skiff, running
south toward brighter skies, our last shot at finding a tarpon and
feeding it with feathers. I'd packed away all our conventional
gear, and the live well was empty, so the only rod on the boat
was a ten-weight, my muskie rod, rigged with fifty-pound leader
and my favorite tarpon fly.

We ran past Indian Key Cut, through the Wheel Ditch,
and farther on past Lower Matecumbe Key, past the big bridges,
shock of blue sky ahead of us. In the wake of the storm the air
was still and humid. There were no boats around, a rarity for an
Islamorada May afternoon.

We ran farther, to a spot we'd fished all week without seeing
much of anything, and, as we idled, we ran over several large
tarpon.

"They're here," I said. Parker pulled the ten-weight from the
gunwale.

Up on the platform, I pushed us through six feet of slightly
stained water. The clouds parted and we found ourselves in
direct sunlight, light breeze, heat drying the skiff quickly. I could
smell the evaporation, could feel the sun burning the tops of my

hands. It was as if the storm had never happened. I cleaned my fogged sunglasses as Parker readied himself on the bow.

The first group of three floated parallel one another, like logs. I called them out and poled carefully in their direction. When we were about seventy feet away, I told Parker to cast to the nearest tarpon.

His cast was on target, landing a dinner-plate away from the tarpon's nose. He slid the fly once and the tarpon awoke, followed his fly as he stripped it.

"She's on it," I said.

He kept stripping, and the big tarpon tracked his fly but didn't take, turning off at the last moment.

"I thought she was gonna eat it," Parker said.

"She wanted it. That's what happens when you make the cast."

I poled farther down the flat. Parker adjusted line. I could sense his confidence rising—as I had after he'd made that good cast at the laid-up giant with Rich, years prior. Now he stood on the bow with his shoulders wider, a little taller somehow, puffed up, ready. We spooked a large permit that Parker considered casting to, but he held off.

Off the bow, a large tarpon, laid-up and facing us, its tail just beneath the surface and its business end a bit deeper.

"Big single, twelve o'clock, ninety feet. Got it?"

"Got it."

"Let me get you closer."

I poled within seventy, sixty-five, sixty feet, nervous about spooking the fish in the calm but wanting to get in Parker's range.

"Go ahead."

Parker took a few false casts: tight loops and good line speed. He stopped the rod tip high, and line shot forward. His fly landed just off the tarpon's snout, a perfect cast. It sank a few inches.

"Slow," I said.

Parker stripped the fly to life: a long, measured, foot-long strip.

The tarpon quivered, kicked its tail, sunk beneath the fly, and tracked it. I could see its giant eyes watching the fly.

"Here she comes," I said. "Slow. Slowww."

The tarpon rose beneath Parker's fly. A slight crack of its mouth, a subtle turn, and the fly disappeared.

Feeling the weight of the fish, Parker set the hook, and the tarpon launched from Florida Bay.

I shouted choice words I shouldn't repeat. The tarpon raced and jumped twice more, the last a head-over-tail flip with Parker's fly sling-shotting back toward the skiff.

I hopped down from the platform and hugged Parker, who was holding his arms aloft like he'd just won The Masters. In a sense he had. We sat in the sun and recounted every second.

"What a way to end the trip," I said. "That was a monster."

"It was slow motion," he said, "until she felt the hook."

We motored to a nearby beach, anchored, and jumped in. The air and water were the same temperature. I pulled two beers from the cooler. It was easy to float with the bay's buoyancy, and it felt good to close my eyes and absorb the heat. We sat in the shallows sipping beer, talking tarpon. I could not believe what had just happened. I relived my first fly-rod tarpon in my mind. Somehow, they were all connected. I was proud of my friend for his persistence, for making the cast.

Parker checked his phone and messaged a few fishing buddies.

"How does it feel?" I asked.

"Like a dream," Parker said. "It'll take a while to sink in."

We kept talking about the tarpon. The tide was going out. We finished the beer and kept on talking. For a little while, we forgot about our drive home.

SERPENTINE

This place is a frog's nightmare. Bank-eroded trees cling to the shoreline in various stages of decay, providing perfect ambush spots for finned predators. Farther out in this stagnant river, lily pads bejeweled with yellow flowers contrast deep water pockets the color of tea. Milfoil and other spindly weeds crowd the channel, which at its deepest reaches only four or five feet. All is peaceful now but I'm hoping to change that. I'm chucking a popper fly from my canoe, trying to tempt a fat summertime largemouth to the surface.

I'm fishing early to avoid the heat, when largemouth bass get lethargic. I paddle past a warped wooden dock and an abandoned camp. I'm trying to sell my homemade fly as a dimwitted frog, so I aim my casts as close to bass cover as possible. This time it lands with a splat near a branch that points like a gnarled finger, the kind of presentation that would send skittish trout zooming to the next town over. But this is far from blue ribbon trout water, and my fly's splash-landing might be a bass's dinner bell.

I rid the fly line of slack and impart a long, sharp strip. From its concave foam head my fly produces an audible *gah-luump* The boil settles. I remind myself to stay patient. Summertime largemouth are notoriously lazy and shouldn't be fished in a rush. I learned this as a boy, fishing here, around these same

docks and deadfalls. I recognize the stump where the river turns
west—I've fished around it since I was ten, and I can remember
some of the bass I've pulled from the area. I slow the cadence
of my retrieve to match my quarry's temperament: *pop*, pause,
pop, pause. I watch the fly settle after each strip and anticipate an
explosion that doesn't come, at least not yet.

Largemouth bass lack the glamour of other large-growing
sport fish, and this is partly why I love them. They're the fish of
the culvert, the golf course pond, the mud puddle behind the
Walmart. They thrive in nearly every state and tolerate warm,
oxygen-depleted waters like the one I'm fishing this morning, the
Serpentine River.

A wader-clad trout enthusiast might raise his or her nose
at bass; they're certainly an overlooked opportunity here in
Maine. My choice to target bass in the heat of summer is partly
an ethical one—by now most of my trout spots are too warm
to fish. Temperature-tolerant bass, on the other hand, offer the
topwater angler a willing summertime target.

Bass are not as aesthetically pleasing as, say, brook trout or
rainbows. They sport large heads with bulging eyes, football-
shaped bodies camouflaged by mottled olives and browns and
yellows. They're often associated with the run-and-gun, high-
octane nature of tournament bass fishing, which I'd like to stay
far away from. Tossing frog or mouse flies from a quiet canoe
might be the antithesis of the tourney scene, and it can be damn
productive fishing.

If trout anglers were to wade this river—an act I would love
to witness—they could expect to emerge wrapped in strands of
invasive weeds. Their wading boots would stink of dead plant
material and muck. Such is the nature of bass environs—they
live where other gamefish can't, feeding on baitfish, crayfish,
frogs, and whatever else they can fit their oversized mouths

around. For their resilience, bass are rewarded a long lifespan, up to twenty years in some instances, along with minimal natural predators. The eagerness of large bass to garbage a well-placed frog imitation is what has me fishing this river methodically, optimistic despite my slow start.

It's amazing how familiar water imprints memory: here, near overhead power lines and an expanse of lily pads, is where my childhood friend, Evan, caught a seven-pounder well after sunset, some twenty years ago. He had said, "Watch this," and then chucked an eight-inch striped bass lure as far as he could. It was not unusual for Evan to try questionable things; in his senior picture he bit down on an axe handle. I didn't think much of his cast. It was so dark I couldn't see the lure, but I heard the distant splash, and then his surprise when his retrieve was interrupted. I take a few casts but can't summon his luck.

Paddling farther, I pass the camp that once belonged to my grandparents. It's painted a different color now—gray instead of red—but the structure still looks familiar, though the screened in porch is gone. I learned to fish from their dock: red and white bobbers, squirming nightcrawlers, my grandmother calling me in to dinner through the screened in porch, and me pretending not to hear her calls, hoping for another bite.

The only time my grandmother, Annie, went fishing with us, all four-foot-ten of her, was back when my grandfather owned a small white fishing boat fixed with a janky outboard. Grandma, Grandpa, Dad, and I idled out of this same river into East Pond, just after dinner, mid-summer, cumulus clouds like mountain ranges in the sky. I was terrified of thunderstorms and lightning and asked Dad over and over if the clouds were coming our way—they were not. It took twenty minutes to motor from camp to lake, and, once we got out to the fishing spot, it was my job to let back our lures, which we trolled at various depths.

I took the job seriously, checked the drag on each reel, set the rods in their holders at appropriate angles once the lures were out. I had just set the second rod in its holder, the old Mercury chugging along and my excitement rising, when my grandmother said, "When does one call it quits?"

That was the last time we took Grandma fishing.

Usually it was just Grandpa, Dad, and me. They were not particularly close when my father was young, he told me later, and they had tried at closeness later in my grandfather's life. We dragged blaze-orange Rapalas on ultra-lite rods and kept every white perch that came over the gunwales. Back at camp, well after dark, Dad sharpened his filet knife on a honing rod and sliced open the perch's pearlescent bellies. I liked to inspect the stomach contents: nymphs, worms, shiners, crayfish, spread and smeared on folded newspapers. Dad wanted to finish quickly so we could go home, and he grew impatient with my inspections. We kept the perch filets wrapped in damp paper towel inside a Cool Whip container in the camp's fridge. The next day, for dinner, Dad would dip the filets in egg and breadcrumbs and fry them in oil in a black skillet, finishing them off with a pinch of lemon juice once they'd browned.

We gathered on the porch to eat our catch, all of us together around the table, the slow-moving river beyond. I ate until I believed I could never eat another piece of fish, and then, a week or two later, we would do it all over again.

The sun is higher now, but the eastern shore is still draped in shadow. It's so easy to lose track of time on the water. Already the air is heating up. I make a lousy cast and my fly and leader twirl around a tree limb. A lucky flick of my rod tip and the fly unfurls and falls to the surface. I play it back toward the canoe, nothing doing. The canoe drifts with the breeze, which has picked up. Wind is the fly angler's enemy, but I don't mind today, not when the breeze aids in cooling me off. I make another cast, this time landing the faux frog near a protruding stump. After one pop the fly disappears—no explosion, just a sinkhole where my fly used to be. When I set, the bass swims toward me and I worry I've lost it. But then it pulls line from my hands and jumps, trying to throw the fly from its lip. It's a good fish, but the fight doesn't last long in the warm water.

A rod length away the bass tips on its side and I notice how poorly it's hooked. The frog fly looks like gaudy jewelry barely piercing its lower lip. I lift the rod high and reach for the bass, thumbing its open mouth, which is a sizable target. I pinch its lower lip with one hand, drop my fly rod in the canoe, and support the bulging belly with my freed hand. It's around four pounds, all head and shoulders, bigger than any trout I've caught this summer. The bass cooperates for a canoe-side photo. I remove the frog fly and revive the bass slowly, which takes a while in this stagnant bathwater it calls home. I wonder if the bass had been here years ago, when I was much younger, and my grandparents were still alive. The bass kicks off into the dark water.

If you open *The Maine Atlas and Gazetteer* you will notice an overwhelming number of ponds, lakes, rivers, streams, bogans. Tributaries. Too many waterways to fish in two lifetimes. So why do I return to this unremarkable, static river, with so many opportunities to explore, to discover, and only this one lifetime? I'm not sure. It's not as simple as nostalgia. Each time I return to the Serpentine, to Islamorada, to the Allagash, I intercept another memory, and a fleeting, irreplicable feeling, and I'm faced again with a different version of myself. I return and remember who I am.

I catch a few smaller bass before the sun crests the trees and the bite dies. My frog fly is missing a leg but still functional. As I paddle back to my vehicle—past my grandparent's cabin, which of course is not theirs anymore, on beneath the powerlines where Evan summoned that monster bass decades ago—I realize I've forgotten sunscreen. I think of jumping in to cool off but recall the feeling of milfoil brushing against my legs. I paddle on, grateful for the chance to toss flies on a dog-day morning to bass I've chased since I was a boy.

A RECIPE FOR CARP

Find shallow flats near deep edges. Search rivers feeding
Merrymeeting Bay, also the flats of the bay itself, because
that's the only place carp live here in Maine, introduced by
Europeans as a food source in the late 1800s. Even though
they've been here for around one hundred fifty years, they're
invasive, like most of us, if you go back far enough.

Watch them and learn. Watch the floating carp sink and tip
down, watch the mud cloud rise around it, the carp vanishing,
disappearing somehow. Look for mud clouds. Not the quick-
dissolving plumes of spooked fish (you'll see those too) but the
slow, ash-cloud-rise of the feeding carp, carp bulldozing for
mollusks and worms. Look for tails. Not the full-on outline but
the not-quite-right color—bronze with pink hues, then the slow,
Queen-wave motion of a feeding carp tail. Like redfish of the
north.

Don't cast at floating fish. Don't even bother. It's
tempting—their O-Ring mouths just beneath the surface, their
porky, bowling-pin bodies. They look easy to fool, but don't kid
yourself. Don't cast at fast-swimming fish either, they won't eat
your fly. Don't cast at the lead fish in a string—spook it, and

the rest will veer too, like geese. Don't take too many false casts (they'll sense you), don't rock the boat (they'll sense you), don't cast atop their heads, or swim your fly toward them (prey swims *away* from predators, a guide once told me).

Wade whenever possible. You'll make less noise and spook less fish. Wear waders (or get duck itch, as I did). Keep carp spots close. Where else can you sight-cast fifteen-pound tailing freshwater fish in 12 inches of water? Cast to slow-sliding fish, the ones exiting mud plumes. Don't strip your fly too fast (or at all).

With rod high, drag your fly, then drop it naturally near the carp's eyeball, fly going away from fish. Watch body language. Quick flare or turn equals spooked fish. Slow turn plus tip-down means *get ready*.

And whatever you do, after all those fishless days (there will be many), all those refusals (embrace them), don't wait to feel a strike. You'll feel nothing.

Watch for the slightest quiver, the head buried atop your fly, the enthusiastic tail kick. This can't be taught: it's intuition, fishy-ness, a sixth sense. Feel nothing. Strip long and get tight.

Add backing to your fly line before the trip. The big ones (ten pounds plus) will empty your reel. Check drag. Check your hook point. Check it again. Let them run after hook set; they'll bend the hook if you don't (as my friend Courtney will attest).

Fight them quickly. They'll tire after a few runs. Anticipate the surge when they first see you or first see the boat. Bring a big net, or, if you forget one, grab the meaty band near the tail. Get ready for a thrashing.

Remove the fly gently from the rubbery lips. Take a few photos. Admire its awkward beauty: large prismatic scales, drooping barbels, powerful paddle tail. Revive the carp slowly, so it kicks off under its own power, back into the murk. Do tell your trusted friends, but not the ones that might give away your spot.

Go home and tie carp flies. Experiment with color and shape and sink rate. Fall asleep thinking of mud plumes and wagging tails, the strip-set and the whining drag.

THE GOLDEN BOIL

Mist hovers like a ghost above the Allagash River. I wipe sleep from my eyes then walk the short distance from my tent to the picnic table, stumbling over a gnarled tree root. The picnic table is cluttered by fly boxes, spools of fifty-pound fluorocarbon, water jugs, canisters of bug dope, SPF 50, heavy-duty pliers, everything slicked with dew. I take a moment to breathe in the morning. The air is night-chilled, and the only sounds are those of the river tumbling by. I light the Coleman stove and warm my hands over the weak blue flame. I search for and find the cast iron skillet buried in my bin of camping gear.

Since my teaching semester ended two months ago, and since I decided to leave my Portland apartment—a bad fit for me, for too many reasons to list—I've quarantined in a camper in western Maine, three hundred miles south of this picnic table. I've always done better with structure, with routine, and, since school ended, I've found myself lost in my head. Camper living is temporary, just a place to be while I find a better place to live, and my friends tell me I should try harder to enjoy it, and sometimes I do. Other times I feel pathetic and wonder why I haven't figured things out yet—jobs and relationships—whatever *figuring it out* really means.

Given the sudden lack of structure, I've looked forward to this trip to Aroostook County, Maine's most beautiful and least populated quadrant, with heightened anticipation. Over the past few years, I've fished here a few times a year, drawn to the solitude, the natural beauty, the lack of angling pressure, not to mention the muskies. It's a different world, this far north. During the pandemic, it feels like a sanctuary. I've started browsing for cheap land in the area, which might be a pipe dream on adjunct professor pay. Still, I like to imagine a small cabin beside a river like this one.

As I scrape remnants of an old meal from the skillet, Parker rustles in his tent and unzips his sleeping bag. I have almost forgotten I have company. Arriving late last night after a seven-hour drive from Portland, Parker had set his tent next to mine. It's his first time in The County. I've done a fair amount of yapping to him—about uncrowded rivers and lakes in the crown of Maine, about the resident muskies that don't see many flies—and now here we are, finally, with two days of fishing ahead of us.

"How's it look out there?" Parker asks, his voice crackly from sleep.

"Looks pretty fishy," I say.

I put some water on then roll my sleeping bag and break down my tent. The morning feels charged with electricity—with the sparks of optimism that ignite the start of a long-anticipated fishing trip. Parker emerges from his small, duct-tape lined tent, which looks child-sized. I can't imagine how he fits in there, except in the fetal position, but I don't ask any questions. He yawns and stretches. I want to start fishing, but I know Parker needs time to acclimate. He's always slower to prepare, and he's not much of a morning person.

Parker makes coffee while I scramble eggs and pour them into the steaming skillet. We eat quickly and quietly, eyeing the river, which runs low for early summer.

A week ago, Parker's beloved grandmother, Barbara Mae—ninety-two and sharp as a hook point, with no preexisting conditions save her advanced age—died from complications of Covid-19. When Parker called to tell me of her passing, his voice heavy, he assured me he still wanted to go north. "It'll be good for me to get away," he'd said.

I felt the sadness one feels when a close friend loses a loved one. I was reminded of my own grandmothers, both of whom I'd been close with, both of whom had lived into their nineties. On the phone with Parker, I expressed my condolences, said the right things. Secretly, I was relieved that our muskie trip would go on as planned. I needed to get away as much as he did.

After breakfast I clear the picnic table while Parker breaks down his camp. I shove our camping gear into my nearby truck, which we'll return to later with Parker's. We've left his truck at the take-out, four miles downstream near the town of Allagash.

Parker takes the bow of the canoe at my insistence. He's never muskie fished before, while I've landed a half-dozen on this and nearby rivers. I'm happy to play guide; I think it will do him good to put a muskie in the net. It's a far cry from tarpon fishing, but we're both just as excited.

We push off from the campsite and fish our way downstream. The sun is higher now—mist rises in wispy fingers. Current sluices between sharp, pyramidal rocks and opens into deeper runs. Behind the rocks foam lines eddy like spiral galaxies. The verdant banks we pass are peppered here and there by devil's paintbrush.

Parker casts at the western shore and strips his fly with erratic bumps. We stand for deeper sections, a technique we've perfected since our first time fishing the Androscroggin for bass, years ago, now. It's not easy in a narrow seventeen-foot Old Town, but we find our balance. We fall into a comfortable rhythm, Parker casting and me holding and repositioning the canoe for optimal angles. It's a relief to shift my focus from pandemic stressors—the isolation, the relational and financial uncertainties—to a white muskie fly darting in the current. It's good to feel hopeful again.

Six years my junior and a foot shorter than me, Parker fits the little brother role, which I'm grateful for since I don't have a biological one. I know his angling strengths well; he's better at feeding fish than he is at casting. And I know his blind spots; his casts break down after a few hours, or when he gets too excited, and sometimes his focus drifts. He's eager to learn and improve, and what he lacks in experience he makes up for with enthusiasm. If he can launch a big, laid-up tarpon—a feat we still talk about all the time—I'm confident he can net his first muskellunge.

"Fish it all the way to the canoe," I remind him when he re-casts too soon.

"I just want to *see* one today," Parker says.

He fishes steadily a mile or so downriver. A group of hooded mergansers flushes and then circles high overhead, wings whistling. The sky is patched with a few high clouds and there's barely a breeze. Good muskie weather. Parker chucks his fly close to the bank and I watch it dance on the retrieve.

"Here comes one!" Parker whispers. The thirty-incher follows lazily for a moment, then falls off. Parker takes a few more casts where the fish had been, but nothing doing.

"Did you see those vertical bars?" he asks. "That fish was *golden*."

"Sure was. Just wait till one eats."

"Baby steps," Parker says, then adds, "But since that first goal's out of the way, I might as well hook one." It's classic Parker—practical and authentic, open to new experience.

The canoe scrapes an unseen rock, jostling us. We take our seats. The river widens, shallows, and there's no escaping it. We step out into ankle-deep water and drag the canoe, leaving green paint flecks on rocks like blazes on a hiking trail. Sloshing through the unfishable shallows is necessary work, but the sound of the scraping canoe is unsettling. I want to ask Parker about his grandmother—where she came from, what she did with her long life—but I'm hesitant to shift our focus. The shared solitude feels more vital than any conversation, so I decide to wait. The Allagash runs cool along my shins. I hold the gunwale with my right hand, for balance.

Back in the canoe we navigate shallow riffles—brook trout water, though I'm not sure how many trout are left here. We paddle hard past yellow kayaks overturned on shore, past a derelict shed being reclaimed by forest. In the distance, an empty logging truck rattles along the washboard road. I wish I could mute the unnatural sound, but it reminds me we are in logging country. Soon we're above the confluence with the St. John River, in a pool beside a steep gravel bank.

I can feel my neck burning. Mosquitoes probe my exposed forearms. Parker's loops are opening up, but I don't say anything. I back-paddle to offset the current's pull.

"Gotta be one in this pool," Parker says.

"Gotta be," I say.

We're a few hundred yards upstream of the take-out. I watch Parker's fly dance below the surface, and on the pause a muskie swipes it. Parker sets but the hook comes out. The muskie dashes off.

"Damn!" he says. "Maybe I set too early?"

"I don't think you did anything wrong," I say. "Sometimes the hook just doesn't stick. That's muskie fishing."

I've targeted muskie enough to know we might not get another chance today, or tomorrow for that matter. Still, we're rejuvenated by the muskie's aggressiveness, so we paddle upstream and drift through the pool again. Parker spots a muskie holding on bottom, probably the one that ate his fly. He casts a few times, changes his fly and tries again, but the fish—a fat, low-thirty-inch specimen—has learned its lesson.

"That was such a cool bite," Parker says. "See one, check. Feed one, check. Now I've gotta put one in the net."

"I like your optimism," I say. We've got a day and a half to make it happen.

At the take-out we lug the canoe up the steep embankment to Parker's truck. My t-shirt is sweat-drenched, my neck toasted. Once the canoe is fastened to the truck's bed, we sit on the bank overlooking the river, tired but contented with the morning's fishing. We scarf peanut butter sandwiches and chug cold water.

"Where to next?" Parker asks.

If we are going to paddle up this small St. John River tributary near the Allagash, as we've decided to do, we cannot bring all our camping gear. There is simply not enough room and, even if there was, the weight of it all would make the upstream paddle impossible. At 2 p.m., an hour or so after lunch, Parker and I load the canoe with essentials: two sleeping bags, two tents, skillet and stove, frozen package venison sausage, two sandwiches, one bag trail mix, two gallons water, two beers for potential first-muskie toast, eight and ten-weight fly rod, one box flies, large net, anchor and rope, digital camera, two paddles, and two life vests. It's a tight fit even after our culling. When we push off from the muddy bank, with Parker manning the bow, the canoe feels more tippy than usual.

"There's a gravel bar we'll camp on, five or so miles up," I say, as we struggle through the first riffle.

"Five miles upstream," Parker says, already breathing heavy, "that's *it?*"

We round a corner and lose sight of our vehicles, which we've left in an overgrown field. Alders crowd the narrow river. The current is slow and powerful—it is hard work to keep our bow pointed upstream. A moderate headwind doesn't help. Quickly I'm out of breath too, and we haven't been paddling five minutes.

I've done this paddle before, solo, with a lighter payload and more daylight to work with. It took me three hours to make it to the gravel bar. I know what we're in for, aware of the grueling task ahead of us. I'm also familiar with the run's deep pools, and the muskies that inhabit them. I'm hopeful the fish gods will reward our effort.

A half-mile upstream we pass a large cabin on the eastern shore, the last sign of civilization. Then it's only forest—spindly spruce leaning out over tannic water; bank-eroded birch; well-worn moose trails. Mercifully, we enter a slow stretch full of floating grass, as though a thunderstorm has ripped through and churned things up. We make good time, paddling through the dead water. I am suddenly aware of the heat, the day pivoting from chilly to warm to downright hot. It must be 80 degrees. I take a swig of lukewarm water. I dip my hat in the river. Cool rivulets run down the back of my neck. I grab my paddle and dig.

"You alive up there?" I ask.

"Oh yeah—just taking it all in," Parker says.

The first rapids we come to are low and too difficult to paddle. We step out and I lead the canoe upriver. The river runs waist-high for me, nearly chest-high for Parker. It is slow and difficult work, but the cool current is a welcome respite from the heat. I probe the river bottom with my wading shoes, searching for stable footing. It feels as if I'm in some sort of rehabilitation tank, my legs working hard against the ceaseless current. I'm not sure how long it takes us to walk the first rapid—fifteen, maybe twenty minutes. It feels like an hour.

In a quiet tail-out above the rapid, we hop in the canoe bringing too much water in with us. The river deepens and we paddle on. A small mountain juts up to our west, so startlingly green it appears photoshopped against a cerulean sky.

I expect a moose at every turn, but they must be bedded down in the afternoon heat. As we paddle farther north, our adventure seems at once fitting, in perfect keeping with the tone of the year—here we are working upriver, wading rapids and carrying only what's essential. Here we are on the hunt for an improbable fish in the strangest, most isolating year of our lives.

Another dead-water stretch: white birches and massive pines line the steep bank and above them cedars cling precariously to the eroded hillside. Again, we find grass floating everywhere. I wonder how the low water will impact our fishing.

We arrive at the second set of rapids, a complicated cribwork of whitewater and exposed rocks. We walk the shallows, me long lining the canoe and Parker steadying the stern. We walk the third, fourth, and fifth rapids. My legs wobble. Parker slogs behind diligently. We haven't spoken for an hour. Above the fifth rapid, we sit in the canoe and rest a few minutes, the angled sunlight scattered by the shoreline trees. Parker tears open the bag of trail mix and I grab a handful for myself.

"We've gotta be getting close," Parker says, almost as a question, which is his polite way of asking when the hell we'll get where we're going.

"Getting there," I say, though we still have a few miles to go.

We're nearing the run's fishiest pools—places I've moved or hooked muskies in the past, with each fish, each fight, seared into my memory. A half hour above the fifth rapid we beach the canoe and wade a sweeping pool that runs the length of an enormous downed spruce. We both take casts. The casting motion—twisting my torso, extending my right arm to shoot the heavy line—stretches me out from the hunched-over paddling.

By 5:30 p.m. we're nearing the camping spot. I remind myself to hydrate. Parker stands and casts through a few pools. I'm nervous that the low water has pushed the muskies deep or made them grumpy. "We'll find 'em," I say, after another fishless pool.

We navigate more riffles, then enter a deep, dark pool with alder branches tickling the river.

"I know you're fried, but try a few shots in here," I say. "Then we'll knock out the last bit of paddling."

I drop anchor and tie off the rope. Parker stands slowly, groaning like an old man after a long flight. He peels line into the canoe, then casts to the left bank. Loose line wraps his shoe, shortening his cast.

"Get it right next to shore," I say.

His second cast is perfect. The white fly settles softly a few inches from alders. Current sweeps his fly down-pool. He starts his retrieve. The sun is behind us, so that Parker is backlit and the riverbank beyond him glows. It would make a heck of an image—I try to find my camera bag, to snap a photo in the perfect light—but my bag is buried beneath tents and sleeping bags.

When I glance up, Parker's looking downstream, at what exactly I'm not sure. Instinctively I swivel my head back toward his fly.

A golden boil erupts where his fly should be.

"Hit him!" I yell.

Parker strips and his hook finds purchase. The muskie darts toward us. Parker strips line to stay tight. Twenty feet away, the muskie jumps—a tail-walking, gill-shaking tarpon leap. It surges and jumps again, then swims deep. Parker's fly line slices upriver.

"Ho-leeeeee shit!" Parker says. His 8-weight doubles over. I grab the net and extend the handle. When the muskie sees the net, it turns and splashes the canoe with its tail kick. A few moments later Parker has the muskie at the surface. He guides it into the net.

"Yeah buddy!" I holler.

Parker drops his rod in the bow and looks at me in astonishment. I lift the net so he can see his catch; we both start

Parker's first muskie, after a long day of paddling.

laughing. I lean forward and hand him the net, then lift anchor and paddle to shore.

I beach the canoe on a rocky point and dig through our shit to find my camera. Parker wades in and I photograph him holding his first muskie. Sharp evening light flaunts the muskie's golden flank. Parker supports the muskie with its open mouth facing the current. We watch it revive, then kick off slowly, gliding over the bottom and disappearing into the deep pool from which it had risen.

Parker looks up at me, big silly grin on his face. "Well, I'm good," he says. "Might as well paddle back!"

"Hell of a first muskie," I say. "Those jumps. Man, was I nervous."

"Not as nervous as me," he says.

We sit in the canoe for a while, not doing much, not saying anything. What is there to say, in a moment like this? I'm grateful for the river and to Parker for being here with me. I look back to the spot where the muskie had boiled. The river is placid, unchanged.

I remember the victory beers. I dig for them, crack them open, and hand one to Parker. We toast his first muskie. I'm not a beer drinker, but this one tastes pretty damn good.

We push off and, in our post-muskellunge reverie, paddle through several fishy-looking pools. I remind myself that we'll hit them tomorrow, on the way back down.

"By the way—what the hell were you looking at when that fish ate?" I ask.

"I don't even remember," Parker says, "but I'm glad you were paying attention."

We laugh, and for our last stretch of upstream paddling we move faster than we've moved all day.

At the gravel bar, we offload our gear and set up camp. It's going on 8 p.m. As the light drops—which happens slowly, the sky controlled by the subtlest dimmer switch—mosquitoes arrive. I'm too tired to swat them. Parker sits on a sandy knoll above the river, sun- and muskie-dazed, chewing his sandwich and gazing downstream. He digs in his dry bag, pulls out a bottle of Tylenol. I take a few casts through a nearby run and then climb the bank and sit next to him.

"Hard to believe we woke up on the Allagash this morning," I say.

"That was *today?*" Parker says.

We retire to our tents. I'm wrecked, with no regrets—it's the best kind of exhaustion. As I'm drifting off to sleep, Parker says, from his tent, "Man, that was one hell of a fish."

"Sure was," I say. "Congrats, man. We'll get after them tomorrow."

When I wake before Parker, a mob of mosquitoes wait on my tent's screen door. I step out, relieved when they show no interest in feeding. Hearing me approach, a beaver slaps its tail. The canoe rests right where we'd left it. Beyond the canoe, a narrow riffle extends from the gravel bar and from it comes an explosion. A fallfish flies and lands on the opposite shore. I see it with my own eyes: the six-inch silver baitfish kicking and flopping on land, while a juvenile muskie searches the riffle: *Where did my breakfast go?* The muskie disappears. The fallfish flops back in and bolts upstream, saved by instinct and a bit of luck.

Parker wakes. We eat trail mix and chug water. Parker's head is pounding. He eats more Tylenol. "Didn't drink nearly enough water yesterday," he says.

"Sounds like a muskie hangover," I say, "and there's only one cure for that."

Back on the river, we find our rhythm quickly. We turn the first bend. The current carries us. I use my paddle as a rudder, steering as Parker casts. It is almost too easy. We round another corner, race through a shallow riffle.

"Moose!" Parker whispers.

Eighty or ninety yards downstream, a mature cow stands knee-deep in the river. I back-paddle to shore and grab some alder branches. It's as if I'm viewing a still-life in real-time: a bar of golden light shatters around the moose. I look for my camera bag, which is buried again. The big cow looks over her shoulder. Her calf, maybe a month old, toffee colored, steps awkwardly into the river, followed closely by its twin. They stumble and prance toward their mother. I'm reminded of the cow and calf my father and I watched here, on this same river, years back. The cow leads her calves safely through the river and into the forest. When we arrive at their crossing, the water is churned up, and grass bits float downstream.

"All that floating grass yesterday, I bet that was from moose feeding," Parker says, and I realize he's right.

Parker fishes the deep runs, eddies, swirling pools. From my seat in the stern, I notice him watching his fly intently—hunched—nearly leaning out of the canoe, as if willing another muskie to eat.

We target the best looking runs, especially the ones we skipped yesterday. Parker rolls a large muskie in a current seam, then sets too early on a smaller one a few pools later.

"You should take some shots up here," he says, but I decline. I'm enjoying my role. There's satisfaction in watching the action unfold from a close distance. A few miles downstream already, we stop to stretch along a pebbly beach.

"May as well cook up that sausage," Parker suggests. I'm all for it. As Parker cooks, I rehydrate, use the facilities, pull a leech from my shoe. When the sausage is ready, we eat right from the skillet. It's perfectly cooked, decadent even, after bland peanut butter sandwiches and trail mix. We take our time. There's plenty more muskie water ahead, and no competition to rush us. Parker comments on the beauty of the river, on how strange it feels to cast big flies through runs that look like classic brook trout water.

As we stand there, eating and talking, with the river ambling past, I ask Parker about his grandmother.

She was from Millinocket, he tells me. Worked as a nurse at a retirement home in Portland. Family called her "Grambo" because she used to shoot pigeons with a pump-action BB gun. Drank double gin martinis, two olives, out of a yogurt cup.

"Can't make that shit up."

"Nope," Parker says. "She loved to eat brook trout," Parker tells me. "She never quite understood my catch-and-release tendencies."

I wonder what Grambo might say about Parker's first muskie.

We talk about the virus, about our dating lives, our work frustrations, circling back to the blessing of grandparents.

"She always said she'd live to 105," says Parker, "and we believed her. There was no reason not to."

"She sounds like quite the character. Wish I'd had the chance to meet her."

We finish all the venison—too much, probably, but it's nice to indulge. The meat provides a needed shot of energy.

"You sure you don't want the front?" Parker asks, as we drag the canoe to deeper water.

"I'm sure," I say, and in a few minutes we're fishing again.

The wind kicks up from the south—a headwind—but still it's much easier navigating with the current behind us. We paddle through whitewater sections we'd waded yesterday, scraping bottom here and there, making good time. We hydrate often.

At one turn, we nearly overtake a doe in the river. The doe sees us, her ears prick, but she doesn't move; she can't. Her spotted fawn suckles beneath her. We back-paddle and wait until the fawn has finished feeding. It takes a few minutes. When it's finally satiated, it unlatches, and the doe leaps up the western embankment. The fawn stumbles after, bleating.

Soon we're in dead-water with firs and birches leaning at precarious angles from the bank; it won't be long before the river claims them. We both stand for the slow water. I have a perfect vantage point should something follow Parker's fly.

Half-exposed root balls jut from the bank; tangled bushes rise from the river like mangrove clumps. We pass a beaver dam. Parker works the structure methodically. He throws a backhand shot behind a submerged birch. On his first strip, a muskie appears—it's just *there*—and his fly vanishes. Parker strip-strikes too quickly—swing and a miss.

"Where the hell did that thing come from?" he asks.

"Not sure, but let them eat it, you're setting too early."

"I know," Parker says.

Wind pushes the bow upstream and I paddle hard to offset it. We cross the river and Parker works the opposite shoreline. A feeder creek trickles in, and Parker lands his fly at the mouth. I am watching over his shoulder—one strip, two strips, and a large muskie charges and eats in a violent swirl. Parker is tight for a millisecond, but the fly comes out. The muskie searches for its lost meal.

"Get it back in there!" I say, and Parker makes an awkward backhand cast. He slides the fly once and the muskie finds it; his fly nearly tickles its snout.

Parker bumps the fly. I watch as saddle hackles pulse, then relax. The muskie accelerates and sucks it in, as delicately as a bluegill inhaling a jig. The fish turns and Parker hooks it. It's bigger than his first one. Line vanishes under the canoe. Parker clamps down. The tug of war lasts about thirty seconds. Parker loses the muskie a few seconds before I can net it.

"I've never seen anything like that," I say. "Ate the fly twice."

"Barely sipped it the second time," Parker says. We're both so thrilled by the action, by the viciousness of the muskie's bites, that landing another one feels far less important.

We move through dead water; through pocket pools and riffles, dragging the canoe a few more times over shallow bars we can't avoid. In a deep, boulder-studded pool, Parker misses another muskie. He's so amped that he pulls the fly from the muskie's still-open mouth. I don't blame him. I'm fired up too—I expect a bite on nearly every cast.

On another day I might ask to take shots up front, but not today. I'm in awe of these fish, and proud of Parker for feeding them. He's already put one in the bag—a trip-sealing muskie—and I'm grateful for the days we've been gifted. Seven bites, to be exact. A week's worth of action in one early-summer's day.

A light drizzle greets us back at our vehicles. I'm tired, sunburnt, I stink to high hell, could use a hot shower, but I'm reluctant to leave. We haul our gear up the muddy embankment, stow it in our trucks, then fasten the canoe to my Silverado for the long ride south.

My mind pivots from wilderness mode—from the hyper-acuity of muskie hunting—to thoughts of what awaits me back in the peopled world. For a while I've forgotten the virus, the growing uncertainties in my life, camper life and the endless Craigslist apartment search. It's been a welcome retreat, and I'm sad for our trip to end.

Parker follows me as we drive through Allagash, past Tylor Kelly Camps, the road snaking beside the rocky St. John River, on through St. Francis, into Fort Kent, where we stop to gas up. Inside the Irving truck stop, some locals wear masks and some don't. I hit the restroom and wash my face. I notice paddle blisters on my calloused hands.

Before we leave the pumps, Parker walks over. He hands me a cold water from his cooler. It's a strange place to say goodbye after two days together in the wild.

"I'll follow you to the highway," he says, "then I might take the lead since I have to drive all the way south. Cait's gonna have dinner ready for me."

"Thanks for making the effort to come up. It'll take me a while to process everything we just saw."

"You're telling me," Parker says. "Thank you for paddling me around."

"It was fun to watch," I say. I tell him to call me when we're back in cell range.

I pull out from the Irving, hang a right on Route 11 South. The driving lulls me nearly to sleep, so I open my windows and turn on the radio. Finding only pop-country and French-speaking stations, I choose the latter. I finish the cold water quickly. I look at the clock on my dash and run the calculation—8:30 or 9 p.m. before I'm back at my camper in the western Maine woods.

On 95-South, near Medway, my cell phone lights up in its dashboard holder. It's Parker. In his contact photo he's holding an oversized snook.

"We there yet?" I answer.

"Almost," Parker says. There's a long pause.

"I keep picturing that golden boil."

"I keep thinking about the fish that ate twice," Parker says.

We talk for an hour. Afternoon moves into evening. *Can you imagine?* we ask each other—*what we'd find if we kept paddling up that tributary?* What it would be like to ice fish the deadwater? To throw a mouse fly behind those downed trees? To spend a full week up there, at the height of the season? *Can you even imagine?*

At some point in our conversation, a truck pulls close, flashes its lights. The driver honks the horn, then moves into the passing lane.

"Nice canoe you got there," Parker says, speeding past.

"Drive safe," I say, and we hang up. My phone goes black.

I'm unsure what I'll find when I get back to the camper, unsure where I'll live next, unsure what the rest of the year might bring, or the years following. I think of Parker's grandmother—Grambo—hurtling down the highway in her green VW Beetle. I keep the windows down, find an old rock station when I get close to Bangor.

I replay the trip's still-frames in my mind: the moose and her calves, the nursing fawn, the muskie, and the golden boil. The images keep me awake. I know I'll retain them somewhere safe. I know I'll revisit them, again and again, on long, dark rides like this one.

THE FRONT SEAT

The big brown sips my fly from the surface film of the
Kennebec. My first-ever hook set is clumsy and late. As the
startled fish sounds, my right hand clamps fly line to cork on
the flimsy youth four-weight. Then an unforgettable headshake,
a startling thump and sudden straightening of what had been
a bent, pulsing fly rod. Punctuation of slack line. I'm ten years
old, in the front seat of the Old Town, my dad silent at the
stern. If he'd told me to give the fish line or offered any other
instructions, I hadn't heard him over my racing heart and ringing
ears. I drop my head and cry.

Twenty-five years later we're back on the same river, slightly
north to a slow-moving stretch that holds wild, wary rainbows.
No place for beginners. The Kennebec is swollen from late
spring rains, but lucky for us the water is clear. Dad has a hard
time navigating the steep landing on his bad knees. He's pushing
eighty, now.

"I'm putting you up front tonight," I announce, avoiding eye
contact as I carry his fly rod and vest to the front of the canoe.

"What? Wait a minute. Let's take turns. I'll sit in back and
paddle you around for a while, you know I enjoy—"

"Nope, not happening. Nice try. Stop being so stubborn. I
want you to catch one."

Dad sighs.

I know his turn up front is overdue and that I've been spoiled by having my own Maine Guide and that I've said *thank you* but not nearly enough. I know that despite our ups and downs, we connect on the water, and fishing with me has remained his priority. I know that makes me lucky.

Dad concedes and takes the front seat. I push us off from the landing, bow slicing through floating bugs. A bald eagle watches from a white pine on the opposite shore.

"I still think about that first big brown you lost," he says from the front, his voice wavering. I know where this story is headed, can feel myself deploying the invisible armor that sons carry with them for vulnerable conversations with their fathers, so I try to stay open, present. I wonder if being back on the same river tonight triggered his memory. I wonder how many more evenings like this we'll share.

"As upset as you were after losing that fish, you begged to go back the next night," he continued. "Didn't really give me a choice. You wanted to get right back on the horse."

"Remember the time you gave me our rods to carry up to the truck, and I buried the tips into the side of the hill? I still remember the sound they made, snapping."

"Oh boy. Yeah, I remember. You were a wreck."

"I expected you to be pissed, but do you remember what you said?"

"Not really."

"You said: Ryan, rods can be replaced."

I scan the river and see a dimpling rise downstream and paddle toward it. I remember how he consoled me on the drive home after breaking off that first brown. Gentle but matter-of-fact: *Now you know why drag is important. It happens. You'll remember that fish for the rest of your life.*

Dad continues from the bow: "There wasn't much going on that second night. Remember? But you were patient. That big fish started rising. I'll never forget that. Dark. How ready you were to catch it. You listened and played it perfectly. You insisted we bring it home. Four-pound brown as your first fish on a fly rod, are you kidding me?"

"I wish I'd released it."

"Ahh, you were just a kid."

Dad peels line and casts to dry his Parachute Adams. He moved to Maine from New York in the late '70s and often tells the story of the first trout he caught up here, sixteen inches, *thought I'd died and gone to heaven.* Taught himself to cast, bought an aluminum canoe that's still functional.

In the lee of a small island cairn—remnant of the log drives that once choked this waterway—a big dorsal appears, vanishes. His leader slaps the surface on the back cast. The fly lands right where it needs to, perfect drift, tiny sip and he's tight. A fat rainbow leaps then darts upriver. He fights it cautiously, guides the tired fish into the net.

"Wow," he says, looking into the net and then up at me. "That's a hell of a fish! I didn't realize how big it was."

He removes the fly, which takes a while, then cradles the trout, allows it to strengthen on its own time in the cool water.

Driving home in the full dark we don't say much. It's way past Dad's bedtime. I'll stay over at his place and then drive back to Portland tomorrow, to my new apartment. Crossing the river in Solon, lights from the bridge shimmer in the current and I see the stream where I landed that big brown the night after breaking one off. Tonight, Dad is in the passenger's seat, looking straight ahead. Instinctively I flip on the radio, fiddle with the dial until I find the Sox game.

A few trucks pass but mostly the road home is empty. Bugs splat against the windshield. I wiper them off. A mile or two down the road I get up the courage.

"Thanks for taking me back that second night, Dad," I say.

"Like I said, you didn't give me much of a choice."

THE ITCH

I make it to the river for high tide, then paddle cross-current with my six-weight and a single box of flies. I stow my canoe among high grasses and hop out wearing shorts and a t-shirt. Cool river water laps my stomach. The bottom is muddy yet firm, perfect for wet-wading on a warm, late-spring afternoon like this one. No expensive waders required, and no anglers around, just cerulean sky and the river beneath. Ideal conditions for carp spotting.

Creeping along the weed line to a flat I've scouted, I spot them: five, six, seven carp, all of them porcine and floating. I tie on a weighted worm fly, stand near the flat's edge, and wait for the tide to drop.

This waiting lasts about thirty minutes. A raft of mallards paddles by, lingering for a while, disappointed when I don't offer snacks. On a nearby sand bar, a pair of Canada geese honk their disapproval at my presence; they must have a nest in the tall grasses. Downriver, a pleasure boat drags a water-skier. It's slack tide. The carp don't move. Over and over, I fight the urge to cast, but floaters like these rarely eat. Their flanks range from copper to nearly blaze orange; their O-ring mouths look smooshed against plump bodies.

Slowly the tide begins to fall, and with the movement the carp awaken. A smaller specimen sinks and vanishes; a large carp glides through grasses like a bronze blimp. Soon, fish dig and bubble and bulldoze. Plumes of golden mud rise and disperse.

Carp begin to feed in my direction. I choose the fish closest to me, mindful not to spook the rest. I make tentative shots, then better ones, but it doesn't seem to matter. No response. I accidentally drop my fly on one's head, then another fish flushes when I gently strip my fly. The flat loses water.

This is tidal Maine carp fishing: waiting for brief feeding windows, taking only the best shots so as not to spook the group, and then feeling ignored or rejected. It's clear these fish are eating well, so I know I must be doing something wrong.

What comes to mind, as I wait for another shot, is something my father used to say when I was a kid. After a slow day on the water, he'd announce, "Well, that's why they call it fishing, not catching!" I hated that expression, hated the toxic positivity of it. I had gone fishless! I wanted to be miserable for a while. I still hate the expression. I guess that's because I love the catching part. The bite, the battle, the brief handshake and the revival, the tail kick and the vanishing. I love spooky, paranoid fish best, the ones you rarely touch. I love when fly fishing feels nearly impossible.

A half hour later and most of the carp are gone, save two stubborn, or maybe dumb, ones, sliding and bubbling amidst the murk. Now and then I glimpse a tail or eyeball. I think I see one, but then the vision dissipates, a carp-shaped dust cloud, a river mirage.

Then a carp appears—a real one—thirty feet away, a silhouette cruising left to right along the bottom.

My fly drops beside the carp's eyeball. As the fly sinks, the carp turns, tips, and eats.

I should have mentioned the tree. Reeds and tall grasses line the flat's far edge, but beyond that, farther downstream, a deadfall protrudes into the river. I'm not great with tree identification, but I think it's an oak, or was one.

After the strip-set, the carp shakes its head, as if it too can't believe what's happened. Then it bolts for the tree. The carp gets there quickly, along with half my backing. I give chase.

Firm footing shifts to mush. I'm river-running, then stuck— then running again. Soon the water is up to my shoulders. I hold the bent six-weight high. Twenty yards from the tree I lose bottom and swim a rudimentary sidestroke, cork handle between my teeth, unsure if the carp is still attached. When I reach shore, I reel in slack and, somehow, the carp is still buttoned, among the branches but not badly tangled. After a while, and with great luck, I guide it through the outer branches and beach it on the sandy bank.

It's unclear which of us is more exhausted—we're both breathing heavily. I pluck the worm fly from the carp's lip. Its scales are part prism, part armor. Docile in my hands, the gasping carp with its drooping barbels looks dopey, though I've fished enough to know better. I revive the fish while kneeling bare legged in the muck. My carp kicks off. I wash slime from my hands and let out a joyful holler to no one.

On the drive home I think of another questionable fishing aphorism, one often written beneath social media grip-and-grins: "Finally got out and scratched the itch!" the post reads, as if catching a fish should, temporarily, offset some kind of rising discomfort; as if successful fishing could put out a fire. For me, the opposite is true. I catch a fish—a fine tidal carp, for example—and I want to catch another one, only a bigger, tougher version. I catch a fish and the fire grows.

I want to go again tomorrow, and so I do. Of course, it's nothing but refusals.

That night, the night after landing the carp, I lie in bed wishing I'd switched out these flannel sheets for the smooth ones because they're too warm and prickly. It's almost summer, after all, time to get with the program. I scratch at my ankles, my calves, but there's no relief. The itch gets worse.

Within minutes my legs are aflame, or so it feels, and it's at this moment—when the itch spreads from my legs to my hips, crotch, ribs, and chest—that I think of the carp flat, and the resident ducks paddling by, and the honking geese, and my wet-wading.

Duck itch is the result of microscopic, bird-shit-borne parasites burrowing into ones' skin and then dying. This is not comforting. Google says I should "expect three to four days of extreme itch." In the medicine cabinet I find an expired, nearly empty bottle of Calamine lotion. I slather on every last drop, then return to bed. Pink chalk dries coolly on my skin.

But relief only lasts a few moments. As I wait for sleep which doesn't come, I picture the carp ripping line toward the tree, trying to escape the strange sensation in its mouth. As much as I try to replay the scene—me flailing through the muck, giving chase—my mind returns to the itch. It's all I can think about. I scratch my skin knowing it won't help, but also knowing that this particular itch—at least this one—will eventually go away.

BEFORE DARK

When I arrive at Rich and Kaitlyn's, in Tavernier, Rich is outside shuttling gear from his garage to the Whipray, which is already hitched to his truck. I park my rental car and step out to greet him, shocked by the humidity. It's mid-March, and I'm on spring break from teaching writing to undergrads.

He greets me, and we shake hands.

"I'm sorry about your dad," I say.

"Thank you, man. It's been a lot."

He invites me to offload my gear, so I carry my backpack into the house, which he shares with his fiancé and their two cats. It's our sixth spring fishing together, and for the last few Rich has invited me to stay in their guest room. Staying with them helps me cut costs (nothing in Florida is cheap) and allows us to hang out off the water. I cook dinner for them one night—usually chicken marsala with pasta and good parmesan—as a way of showing gratitude for their hospitality. It's far better than staying at the roach-infested inn on the Islamorada strip, which is cheap enough but often anticlimactic and lonely after a long day doing what I love. It feels especially intimate this trip, staying with them, since Rich's father died last month, from complications of Alzheimer's. I met him once, a few years back, but his mind had already started to slip. I remember his warmth and also his confused, vaguely lost expression.

I drop my backpack in the guest room, which has been made up for my arrival, and then greet Kaitlyn in the hallway. We chat for a few minutes. Kaitlyn is a fitness instructor and works at a local restaurant, and she seems to have Rich's number, seems to balance him out somehow. She asks me about teaching, about life in Maine.

On my way to the door, I notice Rich's tarpon tournament trophies on the windowsill, a couple of fishing magazines on his table, a stack of bills nearby, tins of cat food.

In the driveway Rich fiddles with the Whipray's push pole. We're booked for two days of tarpon fishing, starting tomorrow, but Rich has an idea.

"With these light winds I figure we could salvage the last couple hours this afternoon, if you're cool with it."

"Oh, I'm cool with it."

"Thought you might be."

I know how unusual it must be for a guide to invite his angler to stay with him, and to take him out for a few hours of free fishing. There is always an awkwardness to our transaction—when I hand him a check at the end of the trip, as if I'm paying too for his friendship, but I am feeling less like his client and more like his friend, despite the obvious business component of our relationship. We load into his truck and head north, catching up along the way. Rich asks about Maine, about ice fishing, and I ask about his guiding year. He tells me March cold fronts have dropped water warms, with north winds regularly ripping through, which have made the tarpon grumpy. With the mild afternoon breeze today and the good light, we'll try to find a bonefish, despite our bad luck with them, historically. We pull into Harry Harris boat launch, in Tavernier, with a sign that reads, "Gates close at sunset" and then we're offloading the skiff into the ocean.

Rich's greatest gift, aside from tenacity, is his vision. He spots fish long before I do and sees fish I never see. The only time he gets flustered, truly frustrated with me, is when I can't spot fish he's spotted. He wants a bite as badly as I do, or more so, and we can't get a bite if I can't see the fish to cast to. An example of one such exchange, from a previous trip, tarpon fishing over mottled bottom:

> Rich: OK Ryan, two fish sliding toward the bow, sixty feet, 10 o'clock. See 'em?
> Me: No.
> Rich: Fifty feet! Swimming slow. Giants! Got 'em?
> Me: Still no.
> Rich: Forty feet! Start casting.
> Me: I don't see 'em.
> Rich: [irritated sigh] Gotta get your eyes checked . . .

Or, from a night hunting invasive iguana:

> Rich [spots iguana high in tree]: There! Big green one on the branch, see it?
> Me: Nope.
> Rich [points spotlight dramatically]: Right *there*. Giant green thing!
> Me: The whole tree is green!
> Me: [hands air gun to Rich]
> Rich: [fires] Got him! [giant iguana tips, free-falls through branches, smacks ground]

Once, I saw a monkey outside Rich and Kaitlyn's. You read that correctly. We had just returned from dinner after a day of tarpon fishing. I was stone sober, and Rich and Kaitlyn had gone inside first; I was trying to find something or other in my rental car, which I'd parked at the edge of their driveway. Their home is situated about seventy-five yards from Route 1, with a buffer of trees and large tropical bushes. As I walked to their front door, along the stone pathway, with the outside lights on, there it was, squatting, watching me: a monkey, a few feet tall, gray-brown and with a long tail. It turned and ran then hopped over a fence toward the road. I went inside. Kaitlyn was at the sink.

"Kaitlyn," I said, "I'm going to say something strange and you're not going to believe me."

Rich entered the room, didn't believe me either, was convinced I'd seen one of their cats. The more I held my ground the more he started to consider it: he thought maybe a neighbor had mentioned seeing one, a long time ago. Then we watched a recording from his front-door home security camera and sure enough, there was something, monkey-like, leaping over the fence ahead of me, though the quality was poor, a little blurry, and we couldn't fully confirm my sighting.

"You sure you see something there?" I asked, as we rewound the tape and played it back, over and over.

"I'm sure," he said. "I get paid to see things."

"Good point," I said.

They haven't seen the monkey since, but I know what I saw.

And yet, despite Rich's vision, despite our teamwork and my angling improvements in our years fishing together, I've never caught a bonefish on a fly with him. We still joke about the monkey, also that I'm bonefish repellant. I'm not too bothered by this, given our tarpon success, but Rich would like to check bonefish off our list. He considers bonefishing the purest form of flats angling, since bonefish are present year-round and operate in such a narrow vertical plane, feeding in water barely deep enough to conceal them. He cut his teeth on big oceanside bonefish when he was a teenager. A few days before this trip, he'd texted me photos of two clients—both women in their 70s—each holding a bonefish.

"One of them literally reeled the handle off," he'd texted.

"Enjoy it," I texted back, "because every bonefish in Islamorada is gonna bolt as soon as I roll into town."

Rich responded with a laugh-cry emoji and, "For sure."

Soon we're running the coast, Whipray carving green waves, the ocean expanse a welcome sight for my winter-dulled eyes. It's amazing how quickly air travel and a short car ride get me from frozen Maine to tropical Keys' waters, and so it takes a few moments for my mind to catch up with my body. The breeze is warm, the sky nearly cloudless. I close my eyes and take a few deep breaths, trying to center myself as we race at thirty-five miles per hour over sand holes, past channel markers. We'll have a few hours before dark, hopefully enough time for me to shake off winter's rust and maybe fool a bonefish.

Rich takes us off plane and poles onto a shallow grass flat with tide rushing over it. I make some ugly false casts with the nine-weight, then clean up my line and ready myself on the casting platform, pinching the weighted crab fly in my left hand. There is a tidiness to this procedure, to this process, that I enjoy but struggle to describe. Rich reminds me what we're looking for: muds from rooting bonefish, dissipating puffs where they've just fed, or, if we're lucky, protruding silver tails that betray the head standing, actively feeding bonefish.

"If I spot one, I'll tell you what to do," Rich says.

We're in such shallow water, I can't believe the hull doesn't rub, or beach altogether. Five minutes of poling, then Rich sees a flash out at two-thirty, off the flat's edge, so I make a shot and he instructs me to strip my fly with short, sharp bumps.

"Damnit," Rich says. "Thought they were bones but that's a group of small permit." I try a few shots but the school startles and races off. "You'd have to be Jesus Christ himself to feed one of those things," he says.

He poles us farther down the flat. I'm not sure what prompts it, but Rich begins telling me about his father's illness. He tells me about their last few interactions, about flying up to see his dad, in New Hampshire, when things got really bad; about the last few hours of his father's life, of being with him when he passed.

He describes the challenges of being down here in Islamorada without him, in a place where they'd spent so much time together. His mother is handling it OK, is maintaining their canal-side home not far from Rich and Kaitlyn's place. Rich will do more to support the family business back home now that his father is gone. I sense Rich needs to tell someone, needs to offload the specifics, and I give him my attention.

There are certain things you witness on your guide's skiff and nowhere else. A particularly effective, secretive fly pattern, for example. An overlooked spot where you might find tarpon sliding into a falling tide. Such details are part of the ongoing, evolving conversation between angler and guide, a conversation built and maintained with trust. I've been on both sides, and I recognize our conversation's sanctity. So, when your guide turned guide-friend (or is it friend-guide, now?) tells you about his father's death, in granular detail, you listen, and you keep those granular details between you.

I am so attuned to Rich, to this rare window of vulnerability, and to the complicated feelings entangling fathers and sons that his words evoke, that I must re-focus on our surroundings. Dimming sky, rushing tide, grasses tipped and waving like strands of dark hair, more and more of the flat revealed as the water falls. Rich is composed in his retelling, not shying from the toughest details. His voice is clear and calm in the way of the aggrieved, abbreviated only by his push pole grounding, inching us forward, or holding us against the tide.

I think of my father back home in Maine, probably tapping sugar maples, scraping soggy pulp from a bored hole; or hobbling backward up his stairwell, hauling firewood in his wheeled cart; my father who is always puttering, who cannot sit still for more than a few minutes, unless he's in an airplane or a tree stand.

Rich is talking, and I'm listening and scanning the surface along the flat's edge when a bonefish tail pokes through. Rich spots it.

"See the tailer?"

"Got it."

He turns the bow.

"Let it come closer."

On Rich's command, I take the shot, crab fly plopping short of target.

"Try again. Let him see it."

My second cast is better, but there's no reaction, no take, no blow-up.

"Not sure what happened," Rich says. "I lost sight of the fish right before your cast. That second shot looked good, though."

"Hey, it was a bonefish, right? They must not know I'm here yet. So cool to see one tailing like that."

"It's the best," Rich says.

I want to ask him more about his father, but the tailing
bonefish and the accompanying adrenaline have punctuated our
conversation. We are back in the present as guide and angler.
On the bow, I am an extension of Rich, an accumulation of all
our shared success and failure. Our focus shifts fully back to
the water, to life on this oceanside flat north of Islamorada. It is
extraordinary to witness the bonefish going about its ordinary
evening—just a creature trying to eat, trying to survive like the
rest of us. Rich stakes us and we wait for another opportunity,
which comes a few minutes later.

A larger bonefish feeds along the edge of the flat, pushing a
wake, then tailing. Its tail wags sharply, vanishes, pops up five
yards away, its direction random, at least to me.

"You should try this one, Rich," I say.

"Nah, man, take another shot."

"I want you to take it."

"Are you sure?"

"I'm sure. Get on up here."

We switch spots.

When the bonefish is one long cast away, Rich makes a
perfect shot, or so it seems, an effortless cross-current eighty-foot
cast, one I'm not sure I could make. It's fun to see him in his
element. The bonefish wakes behind his fly but doesn't take.
Rich takes a few more hail-mary shots as the bonefish pushes off.

"That first shot, I threw a little early," he says, making a
teaching moment of a missed opportunity.

"I was sure you were gonna get tight."

"Should have waited," he says.

We switch spots again, and I get a few more opportunities
at bonefish that show no interest in my fly. Rich and I are so
keyed up scanning for tails, pushes, muds, so focused on getting

another shot and feeding a bonefish, that dusk has snuck in, unnoticed.

"Shit, man, we've gotta get going," Rich says. I think of the launch, and the sign at the gate. The sun is setting.

I stow the rod while Rich fastens the push pole. A breeze has kicked up from the east, so that on the run in we're cresting waves quartering port-side. We take sea spray over the rails, but the water is warm, and I don't mind. The sky loses light. It's almost unnoticeable, the slow gradients from light to dark, the way the day gives out.

I have always imagined losing my father quickly—heart attack while chain-sawing firewood behind his home, frantic phone call from his wife, Pamela. Instead, I've witnessed his slow progression toward old age, the gradients of which have been both rewarding and painful to witness. As we race back toward the dock, I think of Rich's dad, about the slowness of their parting. I think of the pool of knowledge Rich has accumulated—details from fishing mentors, guide friends, from his time on the bow and the poling platform, and from his father, who was also named Richard. I think of his father losing his mind's archives as his illness progressed—a lifetime of fish, tides, names, faces—gone.

It's getting dark. Out over the ocean, the night's first stars hover.

By the time we reach the launch, the lot is empty, save Rich's truck and trailer. From a distance, beneath fluorescent lights, the gate appears locked.

"Fuck," Rich says, and I realize we might be blocked in, might need to call Kaitlyn for an embarrassing ride home. I hope our late return doesn't spoil the trip, our conversation, or the trust I feel deepening between us.

Rich docks the skiff; I hold the dock while he jogs to his truck. To my relief, an attendant steps from the darkened gatehouse, hands on his hips, and watches Rich back up.

Rich winches the skiff on the trailer. "Let's go," he says, his words clipped with angst. I run the dock and jump in his truck. Rich shifts into gear, pulling the skiff from the ocean.

At the gate, Rich hands the attendant a folded twenty through his open window. "For waiting," he says. The attendant waves him off, but Rich persists, and eventually the man takes the bill and shoves it in his pocket. He looks annoyed. He opens the gate.

As we idle through, the attendant says, "Was getting a little worried about you guys."

"Sorry about that," Rich says. "That's my fault. We lost track of time."

THE RETRIEVE

The flock arrived late, just a few minutes left of shooting light. Not the mallards or wood ducks I expected but instead five or six Canada Geese, honking and gliding in formation over the treetops. The V flared at my decoys, hovered as if considering a water landing on this tiny pond in Western Maine. I stood, picked a target, and fired. Missed. One of the geese, the trailer, veered slightly from the group. I fired again. Missed. Fired. The slightest flinch, then the goose bailed into the trees like a doomed airliner. I feared I'd crippled but not killed it.

Mazie leapt from the blind and dove into the pond. We never trained her quite right and she—a lean, graceful swimmer, a yellow lab with a magical nose—always assumed we'd killed something. When we missed, which was more often than I liked to admit, she'd swim in circles, searching for the duck she was sure we'd killed, looking back at me as if to ask *is this some kind of cruel trick?*

I called her off eventually and we searched the pond's forested edge until it was too dark to see.

There's a nauseated feeling that accompanies crippling an animal, akin to mild seasickness. I didn't sleep well that night, replaying my errant shot and chiding myself for taking it at all.

In the morning I rose before sunrise and returned to the pond with Maizie, who seemed to have slept just fine, likely dreaming of wingbeats and the sweet smell of wood ducks. I paddled us to where I'd fired the evening before, pulled the canoe on shore, and called Maizie over.

"Find the goose," I said, "go get it, go ahead!" Maizie bounded into the woods.

I stood there waiting. Fall on the air—damp, earthy smells—and I knew Maizie was out there utilizing her superior nose, following currents of scent that I could never register. Five minutes passed. I thought of calling to her but waited. Ten minutes. Fifteen. I feared she'd gotten lost but knew better.

Twenty minutes. I called her name. I worried she'd hurt herself or gotten turned around in the thick woods or that maybe she'd made it out onto the gravel road and—worst case scenario—had been struck by a passing car. It was unlikely, given the lack of traffic, but not impossible—and then Maizie came leaping over a fallen birch, both she and the goose in her mouth very much alive.

"Good girl!" I shouted, and she brought me the goose, her tail wagging.

I killed the goose with my hands. One of its wings was broken, but otherwise it looked fine, would have lived a while in the woods until something—some predator more skilled than myself—found and dispatched it.

Maizie kept nuzzling the still-warm goose. I patted her head and scratched her ears, which she always loved, and then she bounded in circles around me, around the goose, barking and nipping at its limp wings, proud of herself, it seemed. We paddled back toward the truck, loaded up and headed home, the goose resting delicately in the bottom of the canoe. On the ride home I thought about recipes, about whether I would give some meat to the dog.

Fifteen years later and Maizie is long gone, buried at the edge of the woods where deer come every spring to eat fresh grass. She had a nose on her. I still tell friends about the live goose she chased and retrieved, about the wonders of her senses. I tell them how happy she was to present me with an animal, each one a small and meaningful gift. I think of Maizie when the days get shorter. I think of her when the leaves let go of the trees, tumbling and gliding to the earth.

FROM THESE SAME WOODS

November evenings I waited at the window for Dad to return from the woods. When I heard his truck rumbling up the hill, long after dark, I held the curtains open. He always backed into our semi-circle driveway, and usually the bed of his truck was empty. But some nights, gnarled antlers reached up from the tailgate—antlers washed in the red glow of brake lights. How quickly I rushed out to greet him.

When I am old enough—ten, according to Dad—we practice shooting in a neighbor's cleared cornfield. I drop the crosshairs of my Remington .243 over the target, but fire too quickly. I have trouble holding the gun steady. I eject a shell, chamber another, and fire. I hit the target high. My shoulder aches from the rifle's kick. "Remember," my father says from behind me, "take a breath and *squeeze*."

The doe chews buds beneath our two-man tree stand. Through my scope I watch its long, black eyelashes. Dad nudges me after the doe wanders off: *Beautiful, wasn't she?* he whispers. He doesn't ask why I didn't shoot. A few seasons later, hunting alone: a small spike-horn and the coyote trailing it that I fire on but miss. A spindly-legged crotch-horn—gangly as a teenager—munches apples and paws leaves. *Let it grow*, I think. A doe startles herself when she farts; I hold my laughter so as not to frighten her even more. Years without a filled tag pile like cord wood. I wonder if I house the mechanism—whatever it is—that *real* hunters have, the thing that allows them to kill.

> My mother's encouragement—non-hunter,
> Brooklyn native: "It'll happen when it happens!"
> My Dad's gentle skepticism: "You don't *have* to
> shoot one, you know…"
> "I want my first to be a good buck," I tell him.

At the sound of my doe bleat, the buck is curious. Black hooves punch cloven tracks in crusty snow. From its bed near the cornfield—the same field where I practiced shooting two and a half decades ago—the buck walks steadily toward a small opening. My pulse thumps in my ears. When the buck steps broadside into my shooting lane, its antlers appear white against green cedar boughs.

I lower the crosshairs behind its front shoulder, breathe out, finger the trigger, and *squeeze*. Smoke from the muzzleloader clouds my view.

The buck bounds off. I have no idea if I've hit it. Dad, late seventies now, an earshot away, texts:

"That you?"

"Yes! Small eight-point. Not sure if I hit it."

"Stay put. Don't chase. Wait 45 min."

He taught me as a boy that wounded bucks run for miles when pursued too quickly. "Pure adrenaline," he said. "You have to give them room to die."

I replay the shot in my head. I check my cell phone. Fidget with hand-warmers. Scrunch frozen toes. *Shot too quicky; too high; too far back. Wounded it, ruined it. Never going to happen. Not cut out for this.*

Forty-five minutes later, I walk to the spot where the buck had stood. I find no blood, no hair. Nausea sweeps through my gut.

I follow tracks another twenty yards. The buck has followed a well-worn trail—it's difficult to tell one hoof print from another. Ten feet farther, I find a fleck of blood on glinted snow. Then a smattering, then splatter on a downed hemlock the buck leapt.

Where the buck crossed a snowmobile trail, it's as if a painter dipped her brush then flicked a dotted line—red trail crossing white trail. Crushed raspberry red, red like hope.

Beyond the snowmobile trail, at a gap in the trees, I spot antlers in the snow, then the buck's crumpled body. It can't be, but it is. I might feel relief, or some kind of accomplishment, if not for the sensation that I'm in a waking dream.

I leave the buck to find Dad; I want him to find it, too. "I found blood," I say, when I meet him near the field, "Can you help me with the tracking?" I try to keep a straight face, the face of a man that was once a boy waiting for his father to come home from these same woods.

I lead him to the blood trail. Dad follows it, limping on his bad knee, until I can't wait any longer. "Dad, look—" I nod toward the clearing. He spots the buck—rediscovers it—lying amongst Douglas fir. His hearing aids chirp when he hugs me.

"I can't believe it," he says, almost yelling, "I didn't think I'd see the day."

With the knife's sharp point, I make my first incision, near the buck's anus. I remove its rectum, its testicles. I cut and peel, cut and peel, then break through. In my haste, an errant knife prick sends shit flying in my beard. Expelled gas, hot blood. Slimy fascia and a sucking sound when I reach in and remove vital organs. My hands blood-warm and slick, I think of birth. Quills of buck hair stick to my red forearms.

Eyeing the steaming gut pile, Dad says, "Coyotes will sure eat well tonight."

The buck drags easily over hard-packed snow. In the field we hoist it, antlers first, into the bed of Dad's truck. We shovel the truck free, and I hop in back with the buck, holding its antlers to stabilize against the field's dips and bumps.

I imagine the buck's origin as it lies limp in the truck bed: its mother watching over her fawn, spotted and scentless, nursing him among the tall grasses and corn stalks. Beech nuts, acorns, wildflowers, tree buds, blackberries, apples, clover, mushrooms, bark, hemlock needles. Easy spring meals and brutal winter ones, pawing at ice to find any kind of sustenance.

As we near the road I think of shared hunger, my Dad's and mine—which is hunger that escapes or maybe lives beyond words. Motivation to rise early and walk beneath a blanket of stars, these same mornings our grandfathers, and theirs, woke early, hot breath rising like apparitions in the dark.

At the cold storage room, the eight-point buck hangs to drain—*my* buck, which is a strange and uncomfortable attribution. I reach in its hollowed torso and remove the loin. I cut gently, then pull. I break peritoneum with fingertips, pull again; violet, striated flesh flecked with blood.

Dad's cast iron skillet is black as a deer's hoof. The loin rests on the counter—trimmed, rinsed, sea-salt and pepper coated.

Olive oil snaps in the pan. I lower the loin gently onto the steaming cast iron. Meat sizzles. I am careful not to overcook it. Two minutes per side, then we're ready to eat.

We sit down to lunch at Dad's table. On the platter
between us, blood pools from the knife's clean cut. Outside it's
November, midday sun already low, angled, fading. I offer the
first piece to Dad. He chews the morsel, closes his eyes, nods. I
take a piece. We don't speak. We give each other room to eat.
I try to eat slowly—to savor this meal that has taken so long to
arrive—but I'm hungry, and the venison is perfectly cooked.

CREDITS

Essays in this book first appeared (albeit in slightly different form) in the following publications. Many thanks to the editors.

"Rises," "The Sweet Spot," "How to Catch a Maine Muskie," "False Casts," "A Pole Down Memory Lane," "The Front Seat," and "The Itch," in *The Drake*.

"November Light," in *River Teeth: A Journal of Nonfiction Narrative*.

"Ten-Year Tarpon" and "The Golden Boil," in *Gray's Sporting Journal*.

"Pair of Jacks," in *The FlyFish Journal*.

"Heart of the Backcountry," in *Stonefly*.

"The Retrieve," for *Duck Camp*.

"Lost Voices," "For Love of Hardwater," "A Recipe for Carp," and "Sounds of Spring," for *Bangor Daily News*.

"Serpentine," for *MeatEater*.

"From These Same Woods," in *The Maine Review*.

ACKNOWLEDGEMENTS

So many friends and loved ones supported me in making this book a reality. Thanks first to my writing group, six years and going strong: Bill Stauffer, Kris Millard, Catharine Murray, Mary Katherine Spain, Sophie Nelson. I love you guys.

Thanks to my Stonecoast mentors, who helped me shape my writing self: Rick Bass, Sarah Braunstein, Susan Conley, Deb Marquart. That's a hell of a lineup. I'm lucky for the time with each of you. Thanks also to Justin Tussing, Matt Jones, Robin Talbot, Madison Sudon, Jennifer O'Connell, Heather Wilson, Melanie Viets, Stella Skordalellis. Thanks Shannon Ratliff, Michael Garrigan, janan alexandra, Noah Davis, Erin Block, Miles Nolte, Sam Lungren, Morgan Talty, for your support and for creating work that inspires me. Thanks to Tom Bie for noticing something in my early work; thanks to all the editors who have given my work a platform.

Thanks Dean and Crew at Islandport Press—I'm grateful.

Thanks to my wonderful UNE students, who keep me feeling young.

Thanks Katherine, Jersey, Naomi, Dan Sites, Dan MacLeod, Katie Keating, Tim Jackson (RIP), Bob Foster. Thank you, Nora.

Thanks to Rich Campiola, for your guidance and friendship. Fishing with you is a thrill. *Got 'em.*

Parker, for your endless enthusiasm and kindness. Keep casting.

Thanks Em, for always having my back. Thanks Mom, for being my first reader, copy editor, and cheerleader.

Dad, for first taking me to woods and waters. Without you there's no book, or, if there is, it's missing its heart.

ABOUT THE AUTHOR

Ryan Brod is a writer, Maine Fishing Guide, fly tyer,
filmmaker, and educator whose work has appeared in numerous
magazines and literary journals. Born and raised in Smithfield,
Maine, he teaches composition and creative nonfiction at
the University of New England. To connect with Ryan, visit
www.ryanbrod.com.